C. S. FORESTER
and the Hornblower Saga

C. S. Forester

Courtesy of Mrs. Dorothy Forester

C. S. FORESTER
and the Hornblower Saga

REVISED EDITION

SANFORD STERNLICHT

SYRACUSE UNIVERSITY PRESS

Syracuse University Press Edition 1999
99 00 01 02 03 04   6 5 4 3 2 1

Original edition published as *C. S. Forester* in 1981 by G. K. Hall & Co.

The paper used in this publication meets the minimum requirements
of American National Standard for Information Sciences—Permanence
of Paper for Printed Library Materials, ANSI Z39.48-1984. ⊛™

Library of Congress Cataloging-in-Publication Data
Sternlicht, Sanford V.
C.S. Forester and the Hornblower saga / by Sanford Sternlicht.—
Rev. ed.
p. cm.
Rev. ed. of: C.S. Forester. c1981.
Includes bibliographical references (p.   ) and index.
ISBN 0-8156-0621-4 (pbk. : alk. paper)
1. Forester, C. S. (Cecil Scott), 1899–1966—Criticism and
interpretation.   2. Forester, C. S. (Cecil Scott), 1899–1966—
Characters—Horatio Hornblower.   3. Napoleonic Wars, 1800–1815—
Literature and the wars.   4. Historical fiction, English—History
and criticism.   5. Sea stories, English—History and criticism.
6. War stories, English—History and criticism.   7. Hornblower,
Horatio (Fictitious character. I. Sternlicht, Sanford V. C.S.
Forester. II. Title.
PR6011.056Z89 1999
823'.912—dc21   99-36792

To David and Daniel

Sanford Sternlicht teaches English at Syracuse University and is a poet, critic, and theater director. His works of criticism include *John Webster's Imagery and the Webster Canon* (1972), *John Masefield* (1977), *Padraic Colum* (1985), *John Galsworthy* (1987), *R. F. Delderfield* (1988), *Stevie Smith* (1990), and *All Things Herriot: James Herriot and His Peaceable Kingdom* (Syracuse University Press). He has edited *Selected Short Stories of Padraic Colum* (1985), *Selected Plays of Padraic Colum* (1986), *Selected Poems of Padraic Colum* (1989), and *In Search of Stevie Smith* (1991), all published by Syracuse University Press. Commander Sanford Sternlicht, USNR (Ret.), sailed the same seas as Captain Horatio Hornblower, RN.

Contents

Preface

C. S. Forester was a giant of popular culture. This lean, bespectacled, bookish man, a semiinvalid for the last twenty-three years of his life, created a superhero of twentieth-century fiction, the indomitable Midshipman, Lieutenant, Captain, Commodore, Lord, Admiral Horatio Hornblower, Royal Navy. Not until Ian Fleming's James Bond crashed into the literary collective consciousness of the Anglo-American reading public in the 1950s was Hornblower's primacy in escapist fiction challenged and finally superceded. The fact that a contemporary British undercover agent replaced an early nineteenthy-century British naval officer as the nonpareil fantasy hero of the general reading public indicates the shift in values of the third quarter of the twentieth century. Hornblower was a hero for the World War II generation and Bond is a hero for the Cold War generation. Forester and Fleming, respectively, captured the hidden self-images of their times.

All of the Hornblower Saga and several other Forester novels remain in print at the time of the writing of this book. Thousands of readers discover Forester's art through the paperback editions of the Hornblower books each year and then proceed to read the entire Saga and other novels of his, including his finest work: *The African Queen* (1935), *The General* (1936), and *The Good Shepherd* (1955). Ironically, this study of C. S. Forester is the first critical book about this influential writer. Furthermore, at this time, thirteen years after his death, no retrospective article or study of Forester has appeared in a major scholarly, critical, or even popular periodical.

Thus the purpose of this study is to offer readers insight into the achievement of C.S. Forester as a widely read novelist. Also it will introduce Forester to many as an historian and a writer of biography, fields in which he could have made significant contributions to scholarship if he had chosen to direct his primary efforts there instead of in the novel. I do not treat his two plays, his work for children, or his non-Hornblower short fiction in this study except in passing, as these efforts by Forester were limited in number and scope, had little influence on his work as a novelist and historian, and were not examples of his best efforts.

Chapter 1 of this book presents the first and so far only biography of C. S. Forester currently available. It shows how Horatio Hornblower concretized the psychological mainspring of Forester's art: the conflict between the author's self and what he would have liked to have been, between his sedentary, cerebral life and an idealized life of daring and action. In that this particular conflict was one shared by most men of Forester's generation lies perhaps the great secret of Hornblower's popularity.

Chapter 2 treats Forester's earliest work, the hack biographies he wrote under contract to parsimonious publishers to keep alive, the weak, fantastically plotted novels, and the book that brought him his first fame as a novelist, *Payment Deferred* (1926). Chapter 3 shows the emergence of the skilled historical novelist, abandoning contemporary settings and psychological plots for fictional studies of war and the Napoleonic period.

Hornblower is introduced in Chapter 4, which serves as a compendious guide to the Saga. The first part presents the Saga as "history" by arranging and summarizing the novels and stories in chronological order, from *Mr. Midshipman Hornblower* to *The Last Encounter*. Thus for the first time the Hornblower reader is able to refer to a chronology of the hero's "life." Part two of the chapter discusses the development of Horatio Hornblower and the Saga in the order of writing, from *The Happy Return* (1937) through the unfinished *Hornblower and the Crisis* (1967). Part three deals with the literary scope and accomplishment of the Saga.

Chapter 5 treats the non-Hornblower novels Forester wrote during World War II. Chapter 6 discusses Forester's experiments with the philosophical novel. Chapter 7 deals with Forester's return to writing about World War II in the last years of his life. Chapter 8 evaluates Forester's contribution to the twentieth-century popular novel and his influence on his milieau.

Ultimately this study chronicles and explains C. S. Forester's rising popularity as an historical novelist over a forty-year period, from 1926 to 1966, and the continued affection a loyal readership still has for his work in general and especially for that naval hero, who was the first fictional Englishman since Arthur Conan Doyle's

Sherlock Holmes to step out of literature and assume a "reality":
Captain Horatio Hornblower.

SANFORD STERNLICHT

Acknowledgments

Kind permission has been granted by Little, Brown and Company to quote from the works of C. S. Forester.

Additionally, I wish to thank the following persons, living and deceased, for their inestimable help: Mr. John Forester of Sunnyvale, California, who has generously helped me with significant bibliographical information over the years; Mrs. C. S. Forester and Dr. Stephen Troughton Smith of Angmering, Sussex; Mr. William Orobko of Campbell River, British Columbia; Mrs. Kathleen Lynch of Vacaville, California; Mr. George Scheck of Penfield Library, State University of New York at Oswego; and most recently the brilliant staff of the Faculty Computing Center of Syracuse University.

Chronology

1938 *Flying Colours, A Ship of the Line*. European correspondent for the *New York Times*.

1940 *The Earthly Paradise*. Began working for the British Ministry of Information. Sailed on various British warships for background information.

1941 *The Captain from Connecticut*.

1943 *The Ship*. Crippled by arteriosclerosis while on board the U.S.S. *Tennessee* in combat. Returned to California.

1944 Divorced.

1945 *The Commodore*. Returned to Royal Navy vessels in the Pacific.

1946 *Lord Hornblower*.

1947 Married Dorothy Ellen Foster.

1948 *The Sky and the Forest*. Suffered heart attack.

1950 *Mr. Midshipman Hornblower, Randall and the River of Time*.

1952 *Lieutenant Hornblower*.

1953 *Hornblower and the Atropos*. Declined honors from Queen Elizabeth II.

1955 *The Good Shepherd*.

1956 *The Age of Fighting Sail*.

1958 *Hornblower in the West Indies*.

1959 *Hunting the Bismarck*.

1961 *Hornblower and the Hotspur*.

1962 Suffered second heart attack.

1964 *The Hornblower Companion*. Suffered a severe stroke and paralyzed.

1966 Died of heart failure in Fullerton, California, on April 2.

1967 *Hornblower and the Crisis* and *Long Before Forty* published posthumously.

CHAPTER 1

The Storyteller

HE did not win a Nobel Prize or a Pulitzer or any major literary award for that matter, but when Cecil Scott Forester died his obituary began on page one of the *New York Times,* some 8 million copies of his books had been published, and the fictional captain whom he had created, and whom he had tried to dispatch without success from time to time, survived him. Although a commoner by birth, his art had led him to courts and to the acquaintance of nobility. Although a civilian all his life his writing allowed him to walk the quarterdecks of great men-of-war with admirals and captains. Although a semiinvalid from 1943 almost until his death on April 2, 1966, he continued to be a world traveler. Despite illness and adversity, year in and year out he produced his self-determined quota of well-crafted fiction and nonfiction. In 1958, Forester confessed:

There is an acute, if oddly flavored, pleasure in looking round at Naples or Suva and telling myself that I would not be doing so if I had not learned how to make marks on paper. There have been times when I have stood on the bridge of a battleship, when royalty has actually shaken me by the hand. I have had a remarkably happy life—I doubt if anyone could have had a happier during the 20th century—but I wonder whether it might not have been happier still if during those moment I had not felt such a fraud. Yet, on the other hand, perhaps that suspicion of fraud enhances the flavor.[1]

C. S. Forester was no fraud. Rather, he was a person who loved to tell stories, and who, although chafing at the drudgery of writing, enjoyed the imaginative process of creating the illusion of reality out of thoughts and words, a process that, to his continued pleasure, brought him fame and wealth as well as satisfaction.

Forester created an amazing fictional character, Horatio Hornblower, one of the exceedingly great creatures of the imagination who escape, as if back through the looking glass, from the world of art to an

15

independent reality established by and in the mind of the public, like a Hamlet or a Sherlock Holmes or a Kilroy. Hornblower is the ideal naval officer and perhaps the perfect hero in that, indeed, he is not perfect. A strong but kind leader, he deals equally well with the tactical, logical, and training problems of a man-of-war in the age of fighting sail, and with the overriding question of grand strategy in the long Napoleonic wars. Yet he is human, too: often nervous before the opening of a sea fight, occasionally vulnerable to extra-marital love while his wife is safely stowed at home, a bit smug and self-righteous when things are going his way and he has done a pretty piece of work, and, yes, prone to seasickness. Captain Horatio Hornblower is part Horatio Nelson, part C. S. Forester, but mostly just himself.

Forester came to realize his irrevocable interdependency with Hornblower. He called the captain "one of my closest friends" who had saved him from the "life of a cabbage in a wheelchair." Sometimes, however, Forester resented being chained to the indomitable seaman: "I think I have groaned over Hornblower; I have published verses laughing at him, but he does not recognize a rebuff when he meets one. He thrusts his kindnesses upon me, and I accept them with prickings of conscience."[2] Forester summed up the relationship this way: "there is comfort in the thought that I am as necessary to him as he is to me, when all is said and done. We are Siamese twins and the surgical operation has not yet been devised which can separate us. I am not quite sure if I would like that operation to be performed in any case."[3]

C. S. Forester was a transatlantic man, an Amer-Englishman, who loved to sail the great luxury ocean liners between his two countries, who was at home in both of them, and who deeply loved both his native and his adopted land. As a writer and as a propagandist during the Second World War, he did everything he possibly could to bring Britain and America closer toward a cultural harmony and a closely related identity.

I *Youth*

Cecil Scott Forester was born Cecil Lewis Troughton Smith on August 27, 1899, the son of a schoolteacher in the Egyptian Ministry of Education, George Smith, and Sarah Troughton. As he recalled in his self-serving autobiography of the first thirty-one years of his life, published posthumously, his earliest memory was of being on a fog bound ship at sea.[4] His mother was returning to London with her five children, the youngest of whom was the two-and-a-half-year-old Cecil, and leaving behind her husband, who felt that it was time to send his large family home for the education and the welfare of the youngsters. Cecil remembered that the steamship he was on ran aground in Malaga harbor and for the rest of his life the smell of tea laced with condensed milk, a potion served by the grounded ship's stewards to calm the women and children passengers, conjured up the Spanish harbor and the shipwreck.[5]

Presumably the steamer was dragged off the sandbar and resumed her voyage to England, for Cecil's next memories were of a small house in Camberwell, London, woolen clothing, mufflers around his little throat, and the raw cold of February in England, so strange to a child from Egypt. Furthermore the decorators, making the house habitable, not surprisingly, could not speak Arabic, as workers and servants clearly were expected to by the child of a minor Anglo-Egyptian official.[6] There was a warm-hearted Irish maid named Maggie, for comforting, and an overworked mother tormented and weeping over the cracked chilblains covering her hands. She had lived in Egypt for fifteen years surrounded by sunshine and servants, and enjoying official functions and boat trips up and down the Nile. Now there was middle-class suburban London life, only one servant, the cold, indifferent neighbors, and five children to care for the educate without the help of her husband, who could only afford the leave time money for a very occasional trip home. Mrs. Smith found some solace in alcohol. Naturally, her condition upset the children.

Cecil began school at the age of three. By that time it seems that he could already read with ease and write, too, perhaps because his older brothers taught him. In school he was "taught" again to read and write and was, of course, quite thoroughly bored. The school was a council infants' school, like an American public elementary school. Forester was sent there either because his parents were unusually egalitarian for the times, or more likely, simply could not afford to send their many children to private institutions. Also, scholarships for higher education could be won more easily from council schools than from private schools with the greater competition within the latter institutions.

Forester remembered an acute sense of being different as a young child: pushed to school in a perambulator by Maggie, later escorted by his bored sisters, no available father, better dressed than almost all the other children, not allowed to play with children his financially strapped parents falsely believed were not in their class, a Cecil among the innumerable Berts and Tommies, devoid of a Cockney accent, very bright, able to read and write, and highly competitive from the beginning.[7]

All his brothers and sisters eventually won scholarships. Cecil was quite unhappy in his early school years, primarily because he was not allowed to play in the streets with other children. He begged his mother to allow him more personal freedom and to require less study. He even tried sneaking out on a Saturday morning through an upstairs bedroom window, but was caught and punished. In the clash of wills between a mother determined to completely control a child, and a boy's chafing at undue restraint and injustice, the parent won and Cecil had to resign himself "to the amusements of a lonely child indoors."[8]

The amusements were solitary games and, of course, reading. The games were mock naval battles fought with paper ships representing ships of the line, frigates, and sloops of the Napoleonic period; and army campaigns of early nineteeth-century warfare with troops deployed across the map of Europe from Berlin to Moscow. The books came from the local public library around the corner from his home, and in which Forester commenced what he claimed to be a lifelong habit of reading a book a day.[9] First he read the standard boys' novelists of his time, G. A. Henty, Robert Michael Ballantyne, Harry Collingwood, and Robert Leighton. Listening to the discussions of his elder brothers and sisters, he soon turned to H. Rider Haggard and Samuel Rutherford Crockett and then, finally, reached Charles Dickens, whose works he disliked, and William Makepeace Thackeray, whose works he enjoyed.[10] As is so very often the case, the professional writer begins as a compulsive childhood reader developing prodigious skills.

Forester claims that by the age of ten he was regularly reading and rereading Jane Austen, Henry James, and H. G. Wells. James's *The Turn of the Screw* and Wells's *The War of the Worlds* were particular favorites.[11] History received its fair share of notice, with the young prisoner of motherly attention devouring diverse historians like the Roman Suetonius and the English Edward Gibbon's *Decline and Fall of the Roman Empire*. When all else failed, when the supply of readables was temporarily exhausted, there was always the encyclopedia.[12] C. S. Forester became and remained a bibliophile. In 1956 a journalist visiting Forester's home in Berkeley, California, would remark on the fact that the author purchased some 150 books relating to the War of 1812 in preparation for the history *The Age of Fighting Sail*.[13] For much of his life, Forester's bedside reading was a volume of the *Ency-clopedia Britannica*. He read the *Britannica* several times.

Cecil's first infants' school turned out to be an exceptional one in academic achievement. Whereas most council schools seldom produced scholarship winners to secondary and trade schools, his school regularly turned out more than half a dozen winners annually, although no one until Cecil's time had equaled his brother's receipt of a scholarship to Christ's Hospital School. Hard masters and hardworking pupils worked together in a special scholarship class to produce the outstanding result. For years Cecil crammed grammar and math and English literature, and if learning flagged, the cane was employed by the school masters. The young man's mind expanded but his eyesight weakened under the strain of perpetual study and by seven he had to wear eyeglasses, as he would do for the remainder of his life. Although not unhappy, Cecil was small, skinny, pasty complexioned, and continually tested for worms.[14] Then came young Forester's gunpowder plot. He yearned for gunpowder, then readily available at a local shop in threepennyworth quantities. He and a friend saved their pennies, bought several quantities of gunpowder, created a working slow fuse, mined the friend's landlord's garden, and blew the clothes pole to heaven. After the police arrived and Cecil was escorted home for punishment, the military author-to-be relegated his ordnance activities to theory and writing.[15]

After the big bang Cecil's life settled down to a routine of school, afternoon battles with armies and ships, homework galore, trips to the library with armfuls of books, and the very occasional but momentous visits of George Smith to his wife and children in England. With Father there were outings to the Tower of London, South Kensington Museum, Westminster Abbey, St. Paul's Cathedral, the London Zoo, and Madame Tussaud's Wax Museum. Especially enjoyed and remembered were trips to the Naval Museum at Greenwich, where one could see the ships' models and relics of Nelson's and Hornblower's "time." George Smith worked hard indeed to provide for his family and to see them as often as he could despite the enormous cost of the trip from Egypt.

He had much to be proud of and happy over. Particularly, his oldest son, Geoffrey, went through each medical-school examination with flying colors and qualified as a physician about the age of twenty-one. The next son was a star cricketer and soccer player at his public school, Christ's Hospital, and with the family unable to send him to

Oxford or Cambridge, he eventually wound up in the financial world. Cecil expected success, too: a scholarship to Christ's Hospital, Cambridge, cricket stardom, a medical degree at the age of twenty and a gold medal from the Royal College of Surgeons.[16] All things were possible for him, even probable. Indeed, eight years after his eldest brother had performed the same feat, Cecil also won a scholarship to Christ's Hospital. Although his school went wild with the news of the award, Cecil was little moved by it:

I sat in my desk and wished that the distressing noise would end, and when it showed no sign of doing so I withdrew into my favourite mental occupation of keeping the Toulon fleet from uniting with the Brest fleet by the manoeuvers of an English fleet weaker than the two in combination. It was no more startling or pleasing to win a scholarship (twenty among twenty thousand) then to find that there was bread and butter and tea for me, or that the school was at the end of the road. And applause was positively unpleasant when it harassed my eardrums.[17]

However, after the purchase of the necessary school gear, and having taken the requisite medical examination, Cecil and his parents (Father was home on leave) reported to the governors of the school only to learn the shocking news that the scholarship was being disallowed because of George Smith's income, a much higher income than he had eight years previously when his eldest son had qualified for the scholarship. George Smith had only one more day of leave remaining in England. Quickly the unperturbed young Cecil was carted off to a local but fine secondary school: the Alleyn's School, which Mr. Smith's second son had attended. The headmaster was glad to have the brilliant young student, but there was only one place open in the school in a form far beyond Cecil's age level. He was tested and enrolled, but a boy thin and frail even for his own age, obviously very intelligent, and wearing glasses, was, from the moment he entered his first class, marked as a victim for hazing. Cecil endured and survived the juvenile torture, learning humility, control of temper, and the keeping of his own counsel.

From the age of twelve to the age of sixteen, Forester grew from a diminutive four feet four inches to his full mature height of six feet. He also found boxing, and that sport turned out to be his physical salvation. The heroes of his reading had often been boxers, and Jack London's novel about prize fighting, *The Game,* also inspired him. Few of his fellow students wished to risk blows from a fairly skilled six-foot boxer and Cecil now was left in peace. Unbeknownst to the child, or the man writing *Long Before Forty,* his training and experience as a boxer prepared him to endure the intense pain of his later illness. Unwittingly, he expressed a stoic philosophy most useful for the hard times in his future when he wrote in his early thirties: "But there is only one joy to compare with the well-timed straight left, and that is the mad perverse pleasure of standing up to a better boxer and taking his punches and struggling on despite pain and weakness to the very end.[18] C. S. Forester would stand up to pain itself and even to death for the last twenty-four years of his life.

Besides boxing, other school activities of Forester included experiments with electrical motors, writing love verse for neighborhood girls, hazing younger boys when he was older, and founding several sensational underground magazines libeling various schoolteachers. He also studied Latin, Shakespeare, trigonometry, chemistry, mechanics, physics, and other subjects. An outstanding young scholar, he sought full-tuition scholarships to more prestigious schools. None came through in a sufficient amount. Finally the Alleyn's School offered him free tuition if he would stay on for two years. The offer was accepted.

II   *World War I*

During the August Cecil turned fifteen, Great Britain mobilized for World War I. His brothers were called up, his father's home leave was canceled, and Forester remained behind as man of the house. His brothers became captains, one in the infantry and the other in the medical corps; his father served in the Egyptian Coast Guard. His title was Bimbashi and he was in charge of patrolling a section of the shore. Innumerable cousins were in uniform. The family decided to move, partly because the Camberwell neighborhood had somewhat deteriorated over the years, but also because the income had increased. Move they did to Dulwich, a more pleasant suburb.

Primarily for social reasons Cecil, by special arrangement as he was nearly sixteen, was enrolled in a new school, Dulwich College, a fairly prestigious public school, where the young scholar was appalled by the degree of physical violence in the system.

Everyone seemed to be beaten at some time or other; one kind of offense called for the use of a cane, another for an O.T.C. [Officer Training Corps] swagger stick. Small boys beat each other, big boys beat small boys, and big boys beat each other as well, and the masters joined in when necessary. Any offense, from cutting football practice to acting in a sidey manner, called for this form of punishment. What I found hardest to understand about it was the casual way in which it was regarded. Boys put up with the indignity of this kind of punishment without any misgivings at all, would put themselves into grotesque attitudes for the purpose at the word of command, and would joke about it afterwards. They never thought it humiliating; I used to believe in those days that if ever I had been deemed liable to punishment in that way I would never had endured it, and would have fought to my last breath against it. . . . There always used to run in my mind when witnessing an execution the famous words no less a man than Wellington used to a Royal Commission to the effect that he doubted any soldier in the British army could be made to do his duty save by the fear of immediate corporal punishment. Wellington was wrong; it is at least possible that the advocates of corporal punishment in our public schools are just as wrong, and that a hundred years hence small boys will remain ignorant of the appearance and the sensation of a bleeding posterior, and big boys will not vie with each other for the reputation of inflicting the most pain per unit of six strokes.[19]

Forester's Hornblower would be far more lenient than most of the captains of the time he was presented in, when it came to flogging and other forms of corporal punishment prevalent in the Royal Navy at the beginning of the nineteenth century.

The war went on for four long years. Forester expected to have to serve just as soon as he was old enough, become an infantry officer in the trenches on the Western front, and be killed along with so many of his generation. He recalled: "It still hurts me to think that most of those boys did, in the end, meet the fate they expected—most of them were commissioned just in time for the horrible slaughter of Passchendaele, and the ones who survived that did not have the same good fortune in 1918."[20]

With the passing of his seventeenth birthday, Forester went to enlist. Although he only weighed about 135 pounds and wore glasses, the would-be recruit was sure of acceptance. After all, he was six feet tall, an experienced boxer, and a cricket player used to enduring long periods of strenuous activity in the sun. Forester described his induction physical examination:

The army medical examination, I had always understood, was sketchy. . . . I expected the whole business to be over in five minutes. . . . But the doctor who applied the stethoscope to my heart (that was a surprise to me; I had not expected such refinement) was not satisfied. He called his colleague over, who listened as well. They telephoned through to a senior doctor. . . . He too listened to my heart . . . and asked me questions. Nobody announced his conclusion in hearing. Instead I was told to get my clothes on and that I would find my papers with the clerk in the outer hall. And when I found the clerk he was busily writing in red ink all over my attestation form and registration card . . . that I was medically rejected.[21]

Forester was amazed by the turn of events. He pressed for details "I persuaded the sergeant on duty to let me back into the doctor's hall and there I questioned the men who had examined me. . . . They managed to find time between two recruits to tell me that there was no chance of my being accepted for service and that really I should be surprised to be still alive."[22] He left the building "in the shadow of death."[23]

It took the poor young man a long time to become adjusted to the thought of imminent death by heart failure. In fact by the time he had indeed come to accept his precarious lot, his heart and general health had righted themselves, as was later attested by the several medical specialists he had access to as a medical student. It was a bitter and disappointing experience to a young boy of seventeen, yet it was not to be compared with the sudden maiming and death so many of his young friends were experiencing or were to experience in the blood baths of the First World War. Embarrassed by the fact that he did not serve in World War I, Forester much later on apparently hinted or stated that he had had combat service. He was not the only writer to do so. Faulkner did it too. After Forester's death inaccurate writers preparing biographical cover copy for paperback editions of Forester's work, would state without foundation that he had served as an infantry officer in World War I; perhaps they were taken in by his accurate descriptions of battle in *The General* (1936) and *Randall and the River of Time* (1960). They had all come from reading.

Forester was desperately unhappy in his late teens because of the army examination and rejection, the change of schools, his entry into medical school, the sight of his maimed friends coming back from the trenches, and the terrible irony that he served in an Officer's Training Corps, drilling even younger men for a war in which he could have no part. The irony was even greater for although he desired to do his duty to his country, another part of his being cried out against "the whole brutal, wasteful, beastly business. . . ."[24]

Until the writing of his autobiography Forester was unable to confess to a single soul his disgust for the war. Indeed the very purpose of the autobiography, written at the age of thirty-two, before Forester had achieved any degree of fame as a writer, stashed away in a bank vault until death, and never continued although he lived some thirty-five more years, may have been to relieve himself of the guilt he felt when people "tried to sympathize with me for not being in the army."[25] Like any young man in the highly charged emotional atmosphere of nation desperately at war, he felt ready to risk death, but also terrorized that he "might have turned coward if the choice had been open. . . ."[26] The agony must have been intense if even thirteen years afterward he could write: "Even now the relief of confession is inexpressible."[27] Almost every one of his friends had the opportunity to prove his personal courage, some of them in two wars, but physical health would prevent C. S. Forester from ever knowing that one truth about himself which he seemed to have deemed especially significant: how would he have behaved in combat? Thus a man who spent most of his professional life writing about, and perhaps sometimes identifying with, brave men in war seemed to have thought less of himself for not ever being in armed conflict and thus perhaps compensated by, in a sense, keeping company with combat as a correspondent, as a propagandist, and most of all as a writer about warfare.

But, as some of the "facts" in *Long Before Forty*, particularly those related to family background and his very early life, are at variance with records and other accounts, it may be that Forester also chose to use the autobiography to provide future "documentation" for what he had been relating about himself in public at the time.

III   *Medicine: A False Start*

With the army not to be a part of his life, Forester realized that he had a future to think about after all. By dint of family pressure he was destined for a career in medicine, the profession of his oldest brother, who had turned out to be a brilliant medical student and physician. Forester had no great yearning to be a doctor. It seemed as reasonable a career as any, but no more than any other. He was depressed at the thought that he would always be compared with his brother and would always come off second best.

As an attractive young man with piercing brown eyes, nearly twenty years old, Forester began to become entangled with women although he had sexual experiences as a teen-ager. He crassly divided women into two classes, fools and whores, stating: "The fools ran after me and I ran after the whores, foolish though I realized such a proceeding to be."[27] He found women easy fare, necessary, easily manipulated, and not too difficult to abandon when he lost interest. When tired of sex he went camping alone for weeks.[28] Since his male friends had for the most part been lost to him, he did not seek out friendships of his own sex. There might be questions concerning his lack of military service, as young men might compare war adventures, of which, of course, he had none.

At the age of nineteen Forester enrolled for the course of study leading to qualification as a physician in Guy's Hospital. His career as a medical student proceeded from a position of mediocrity to one of disaster. The curriculum was not all that demanding for a bright young man who had had six or more years of good secondary education in science, but motivation was simply not there. The chemistry and physics hardly exceeded his earlier preparation. Biology was a little harder. He looked ahead to his second year and the dissecting room and the operating theater. But he began to slack off, and instead of studying, would read anything at hand. Also, his hectic night life began to get the better of him. He passed his first year examination with a stumble. He was required to take biology again. He passed the reexamination three months later, although he had not cared enough about it to open a book in preparation. Anatomy proved to be the downfall. It is a vast subject requiring a considerable effort in memorization, which Forester was unwilling to make. There was no bluffing here. A half-hour's study, boredom, and Cecil was off to the Students' Club to play bridge, his lifelong favorite card game.

Forester found yet another interest: he began to write humorous articles for the hospital gazette.[29] His turbulent life, his worries, and his academic disappointments re-awakened the storytelling instinct in him that he had from childhood on. It was as if he were moving to the sidelines of medical life, or even life in general, and beginning to comment on it through the written word. He began to need the feeling of having completed a successful sonnet, or finding a story published in a school magazine, and he began at age twenty to consider a life as a professional novelist, not having as yet written or even planned a novel.[30] Solace for failure would not be found in drugs or drink, both readily available to a medical student, but in writing.

However, Forester's life fell more and more into disarray. There were brawls in bars against men with knives, as if he were testing courage again. Meals were ordered in restaurants when he did not have funds to pay the bill, and an irate manager would have to be confronted. Finally he had financial difficulties that led him to degradation. Money had always been short with Forester, especially when he "tried to live the life of a man about town on the allowance of a medical student."[31] He also misused the money his brother Geoffrey was sending him. He could not borrow any more money and he did not have the time to plan an effective burglary. Forester began to beg in the streets of London, singing ballads in a tuneless baritone for coppers and an occasional sixpence. The end of medical hopes came with the School Examination in Bones. He tried, returned to dissecting rooms, put down his disgust, and studied, but to no avail. He was an irretrievable failure. It had to be a life of literature.

IV   *The Writer Emerges*

Forester had associated himself with some writers, artists, dancers, actors, and hangers-on living in Chelsea, London's Greenwich Village of the time. But these contacts were of little use to him. The writers particularly did not impress him. They were generally poets who had a poem or two occasionally printed in obscure little magazines and spent many hours talking about their theory of literature. Forester was never arty. His approach to literature was from the beginning pragmatic, perhaps even bourgeois, reflecting his very strong middle-class background. His family had no creative writers in it and had never known any, avid readers though they all were. Not surprisingly they objected to Cecil's plans. They strongly urged compromise. Why not qualify as a physician first, as Somerset Maugham had? Forester was not to be dragged out of the psychological sanctuary he had created. How could he decide to be a novelist if he had never written anything more than a few poems and a scattering of humorous articles for the hospital publications? Logical arguments were to no avail. He was determined to devote his life's energies to writing, to the point that he "would genuinely prefer to die than to admit failure. . . ."[32]

His future was in his own hands. In retrospect he claimed, perhaps ironically, that at once he determined both to keep to his goals and to maintain his integrity: "Even at that time I formed the resolution (to which I have clung ever since) never to write a word I did not want to write; to think only of my own tastes and ideals, without a thought of those editors or publishers or even of the general public—a perfectly splendid resolution to make when no single editor or publisher or member of the general public was in the least aware of my existence."[33]

Forester knew practically nothing about the technical aspects of writing. To determine the length of a novel, he simply counted words in several of the books he had on hand. Knowing the length of a novel turned out to be quite important, for Forester finished his first novel in a wild burst of energy. It took him two weeks. For years his creative expression had been pent up in the routine of family and school. Now he simply could not stop, but wrote all day long and into the night: "the material came bubbling up inside like a geyser or an oil gusher. There was no need to bale it up with a bucket or a pump—it streamed up of its own accord, down my arm and out of my fountain pen in a torrent of six thousand words a day."[34] Although the gusher was eventually capped, Forester maintained a steady flow of words all his life. He became a morning writer who would stroke between 1,000 to 1,100 words in longhand on foolscap, two pages of fine microscopic script, never indenting for paragraphs for fear of cheating on the number of words, seldom correcting, infrequently rewriting, and stopping exhausted after two hours of intense labor "even if . . . in the middle of a paragraph."[35] A thousand words a day could produce up to four novels a year. Six thousand words: a prodigious level of production.

Not surprisingly, "the work was atrociously bad."[36] A friend typed the manuscript, and he asked her to suggest a pen name, and she suggested C. S. Forester. *C* for Cecil of course, and *S* for Smith. He liked the sound of the name and kept it. The novel was rejected several times and was eventually and mercifully laid to rest. Forester continued writing at a furious pace. Although helped by his relatives, his bills mounted up. When his shoes wore out he was unable to buy a new pair. Forester recalled, perhaps exaggerating and dramatizing his circumstances, that "the most degrading sensation on earth—worse even than the discovery of lice in one's clothes—is the feeling of icy, filthy water leaking in and out of one's shoes at every step."[37]

The new novel was "an awful example of what happens when a young man takes pen and paper and lets his imagination loose without stopping very much to think."[38] It contained a hero who fought in the Turkish Army and served time in a Syrian prison; there was a bit of cannibalism with the eating of a beautiful young woman by her lover while they were imprisoned in a dungeon by her jealous husband; war segments, which the public were quite tired of; and other aspects of bad or mistaken taste. Eventually it was accepted for publication and appeared as *The Paid Piper* (1924). It remained "as painful a memory" to him "as any other foolishness" he had committed.[39] But even before *The Paid Piper's* acceptance, the third novel was already underway. For a while Forester had three unaccepted novels in circulation, and to save postage he took them personally around the publishing firms of London. The third novel was a story of Napoleon and a fictitious mistress who causes him to lose his empire. It came complete with yet another version of the burning of Moscow and the retreat from Russia. This book, *A Pawn among Kings* (1924), was the first Forester novel accepted for publication.

The author felt no joy. His efforts had been painful and enormous. Royalties would not begin to arrive for perhaps a year. He was nearly half dead with overwork and anxiety. Most of all he had come to realize that his first efforts as a novelist had produced extremely mediocre work. His critical acumen was also in the process of developing. He reread his first three novels with a new eye and squirmed. Quickly he put the first of the three novels he had written in six months aside, never to submit it for publication again. In those six months the young novelist learned many things about himself. He knew he could not rewrite and that it was difficult even to make corrections. Therefore his plots had to be outlined thoroughly before he began to write. Once underway there would be no going back in the story. The carefully plotted story would be Forester's hallmark.

In order to make ends meet before royalties would arrive, Forester took casual jobs. He sold rugs, wrote verse and reviews for general magazines. Also he states that he allowed a wealthy woman to take him to dinner and breakfast in exchange for sex.[40] These were surely not the proudest moments of his life.

Except for the few pounds he had earned for his poems, his first money from literature came from a book he had not yet written. His publisher invited him, on the strength of the novel *A Pawn among Kings*, to write a book about Napoleon. Forester was delighted to accommodate since the Napoleonic period had been one of his favorite areas of study. The book, of which Forester was also not proud later on, was entitled *Napoleon and His Court* (1924) and was written in the style of Thomas Babington Macaulay, somewhat verbose and Neo-Gothic. However, the publishers, Methuen & Co., were happy with the first 10,000 words and a synopsis, and they miraculously (for Forester) produced an advance of twenty-five pounds. The author immediately went out and bought a new pair of shoes.

The *Times Literary Supplement* and other reviews praised this book which Forester had dashed off in two weeks and all treated it as a serious work of history; even Forester almost began to take himself seriously as an historian at the time. Now the publishers accepted *The Paid Piper* also and commissioned him to write a book on the Empress Josephine, providing him with yet another twenty-five pound advance. His great anxiety over lack of money was slowly beginning to abate, that is until he received his first royalty check for six months of sales: forty pounds.

Forester enjoyed writing *Josephine, Napoleon's Empress* (1925). He spent many delightful hours researching in the British Museum and was able to give the work enough time to make it a more serious history, although Forester was always a better novelist than historian. Of his first four books, two novels and two histories, this was the one he was most proud of. In fact the two Napoleonic histories would have more influence upon his later work as a novelist than his first attempts at fiction. The emperor Napoleon would become the arch villain of the Hornblower saga, the evil, octopus-like ruler whose grip on Europe Hornblower, like Nelson and Wellington, would struggle to break. Napoleon would remain a character in Forester's writing until the very end of his career.

Concurrent to the writing of *Josephine,* a passionate love affair brought Forester pain and torment. It came to a bitter end, but ten years later Forester felt it necessary to comment on it and its adverse effect upon his early work.[41] He began two new novels in this period but they displeased him and he discarded them both. Finally a novel set in contemporary England began to form in the author's mind. He gave it a little time to ferment and then to settle. This time he would not rush to write but would carefully plan out a complicated but intriguing plot. It was to be about a bank clerk who commits murder and buries his victim's body in his garden, thus locking himself into his station in life and his domicile. The story was worked out in full detail before writing and then Forester began three months of intense but enjoyable writing. When finished he had a book which for the first time completely satisfied him.

Later Forester was prepared to admit that the book, *Payment Deferred* (1926), was faulty,[42] but it was the best book he could write at his age. However, his publishers were not pleased with it. They had lost money on the first two novels, and probably considered that the young writer was good only for hack biographies. They sent the book back to Forester, who was appalled at the fact that his income plans were upset. He was living from meager royalty check to royalty check and a disruption in his publishing schedule might mean starvation. While sending *Payment Deferred* on its rounds, Forester was forced to write two more hack biographies for his original publishers, *Victor Emanuel 11 and the Union of Italy* (1927) and *Louis XIV, King of France and Navarre* (1928). He later said of these books: "They are the poorest work I have ever done, written about subjects I know nothing about, and the sole motive for writing them was the twenty-five pounds I received on the submission of each synopsis. . . ."[43]

V   The Successful Novelist

Payment Deferred was being turned down by each publisher contacted. Money for food was being supplemented by articles and stories for trade magazines and papers such as the *Goldsmith's Journal* and trade papers published by the United Pawnbrokers or the Busdrivers' Association. The articles and stories were pleasant writing, but Forester was a novelist and he was desperately anxious for *Payment Deferred* to find a publisher so that he could afford to go back to writing the novel. Finally, John Lane, a publisher, was willing to take a chance on *Payment Deferred*. Forester would work with John Lane for a long period in a happy relationship. Now only ten months had to be survived while waiting for the first royalties from the new novel. The book was a minor critical success and Charles Laughton, one of England's leading young actors at the time, was signed to star in the stage version, which was presented at the St. James Theatre, London. A film .version followed, and Forester's impoverished early life was over. Hack work was now unnecessary; he could devote his life to writing what he wanted. He began to dream of success in literature, perhaps even honors or a baronetcy.[44] Financial success and worldwide popularity would come, but great honors would escape him.

In the year of the acceptance of *Payment Deferred,* Forester married Kathleen Belcher, a beautiful twenty-four-year-old sports instructor whom he had known for many years. They would have two sons, John and George. The young couple bought a fifteen-foot motor dinghy that they named *Annie Marble* after a character in *Payment Deferred.* They had it shipped to the Continent and began a year of boating through the coastal and inland waterways of France and Germany. Two travel books appeared as a result of the trip: *The Voyage of the "Annie Marble"* (1929) and *The "Annie Marble" in Germany* (1930).

Meanwhile other novels appeared, including Forester's first study of the Royal Navyman, *Brown on Resolution* (1929), and the biography he researched most and most admired,[45] a work that surely prefigured the Hornblower Saga: *Nelson* (1929).

With the successful screen version of *Payment Deferred,* starring the eminent actor Charles Laughton, Forester began a long relationship with the movies from his first seven week visit to America in

1935–36. Although Forester was never fully happy with the film industry and eventually chose to live in the San Francisco area rather than in Los Angleles, he loved California. For over thirty years, except during World War II, he would commute between England and California, living most of the year in California but always remaining a British subject. Film script writing assignments were initially hard to come by. One early assignment was on a Paramount pirate film to be produced by Arthur Hornblow with the writer Niven Busch as Forester's collaborator. Though both writers were dropped from the project, Forester at least got the name for his most famous Captain and First Lieutenant out of the lost job.

Forester's major film credits involved film plays of his own novels or stories, often in collaboration with other film writers. They include "Born for Glory" (1935), based on *Brown on Resolution;* "Eagle Squadron" (1942), based on one of Forester's original stories; "Forever and a Day" (1943), a composite propaganda film by British film artists to which Forester contributed a segment; "Commando's Strike at Dawn" (1943), from his story; "Captain Horatio Hornblower" (1951), from the novels; "The African Queen" (1952), from the novel, and for which Humphrey Bogart won an Academy Award for Best Actor; "Sailor of the King" (1953), a second film version of *Brown on Resolution;* "The Pride and the Passion" (1957), a very fanciful adaptation of his novel *The Gun;* and "Sink the *Bismarck*" (1960), based on his fictionalized history *Hunting the Bismarck* (1959).

In the 1930s Forester hit his stride as a successful historical novelist, rivaling such writers as Kenneth Roberts and Howard Fast, both American master practitioners of the genre. *Death to the French* (1932), published in America as *Rifleman Dodd,* and *the Gun* (1933) contains two exciting tales of the Peninsula War in which the British and the Spanish fought and defeated the Napoleonic invaders.

Forester's next important novel, *The African Queen* (1935) is the one he currently is most famous for, in large part due to the successful film version. Although born in Egypt, Forester had never set foot in Equatorial Africa. His geographical and historical research once more stood him in good stead. The book is incredibly believable and rings with authenticity.

The General (1936), Forester's finest novel, brought him most fame before the Hornblower series. It is a study, perhaps exaggerated, of the peculiarities and ineptitudes of the professional British military mind in World War I. Writing a foreword for the 1947 American edition of the book, the author recounted its bizarre history and its impact on historical events after its publication. For example, in 1938, as a newspaper correspondent he sat with a Czech general outlining the defense of Bohemia against impending Luftwaffe attack. This had come about because the general had read *The General* in his native language.[46] The book was almost immediately translated into German, Polish, Spanish, and Italian upon publication. Most significantly, his German publisher told him that Hitler had read the book and was recommending it to his friends.[47] Apparently Der Führer considered the book to be an accurate representation of the British military mind of the 1930s. He was quite wrong, fortunately for Western Civilization. In 1938 Hitler presented specially bound copies of *The General* as Christmas gifts to important Nazi military leaders like Marshals Goering and Keital.[48] During the Second World War the British traitor Lord Haw Haw broadcast passages from the book to England and the British army at the same time that the British Broadcasting Company was broadcasting excerpts from Forester's *The Ship* (1943), which praises the heroic Royal Navy. It was a battle of books with C. S. Forester the author on both sides. Needless to say, Forester was glad the book was out of print in the United States during World War II; it might have hindered American support for British armies.

Forester was not happy with his life in Hollywood. He went from one writing assignment to another, never quite able to settle down. Finally a personal crisis caused him to leave California temporarily and to take a sea voyage. It was on this voyage in 1937 that Hornblower was conceived. Forester had been signed to work with the great Hollywood director Irving Thalberg on the film "Charles Stewart Parnell," but the two men could not get along together.[49]

As early as 1927 Forester had become interested in the naval wars between 1790 and 1820. He had purchased three volumes of *The Naval Chronicle* (1790–1820), written for and by the British naval officers, and he took these books with him on the *Annie Marble*. He had also bought a history of the Peninsula War and had become fascinated with the character of the Duke of Wellington. The attributes of both Nelson, about whom he had written, and Wellington, whom he admired, fused to help form Hornblower. Most of all, however, a situation appealed to Forester: the position of the "man alone."[50] Forester was fascinated with the idea of the solitary leader who, although having advisors and technical help, nevertheless could only act upon his own ultimate judgement, and in case of failure had only himself to blame.[51] Of course the leader most truly alone was not the general on the field, even one as isolated as Wellington in Spain, but the sea captain on an independent command.

VI   *Hornblower Is Born*

Forester quit his job with Thalberg and immediately booked passage on a Swedish freighter-passenger ship, the *Margaret Johnson*, sailing out of San Pedro, California, for Central American ports, the Panama Canal, and ultimately England.[52] It was a happy and a fortunate trip for Forester. The ship moved slowly from one Central American port to another. It was coffee harvest time. There were fragrance and festivity in the air. A blazing sun during the day, lovely evenings under equatorial stars, and even the occasional storms brought the depressed writer a sense of escape and new freedom. For six weeks he was free to think and feel. El Supremeo, the villain of his first Hornblower efforts, began to take shape even before the hero came into his thoughts.[53]

Finally, as the ship reached the trade winds of the North Atlantic, a hero for a naval adventure of the Napoleonic period began to emerge, and by the time the *Margaret Johnson* reached the Azores "Hornblower began to develop a personality."[54] The philosophy found fictional form. "Hornblower was to be the Man alone that [he] had sought."[55] The name came next. First Horatio—from *Hamlet*, not from Horatio Nelson, said Forester.[56] Hornblower merely sounded right with Horatio. As indicated above, Forester's Hollywood producer's name was Hornblow.

Forester began the Hornblower Saga with the three novels in which his hero is already a captain in the Royal Navy: *The Happy Return* (1937), published in America as *Beat to Quarters; Flying Colours* (1938); and *A Ship of the Line* (1938), which won the James Tait Black Memorial Prize for Literature. Meanwhile Europe was heading for all-out war again. Forester obtained a newspaper assignment to cover the Spanish Civil War in 1937. He had written about the horrors of warfare on the Iberian Peninsula in *Death to the French* and *The Gun*, but now he saw the misery and pain of war firsthand and for the first time: "It was an extremely unhappy experience, during which there was never a moment to think about anything except what was going on around me. Everything was in stark and dreadful contrast with the trivial crises and counterfeit emotions of Hollywood, and I returned to England deeply moved and emotionally worn out."[57]

VII   *World War II and Invalidism*

From England he went to Czechoslovakia to follow and report on the betrayal of that small nation by France and Great Britain, the surrender of the Sudetenland, and the final Nazi occupation of the abandoned country. With the events of September 1939 and Great Britain's entry into World War II, Forester was asked to assume duties with the British Ministry of Information and he requested the opportunity to return to the States to write propaganda films. His request was granted. At the U.S. Naval Shipyard at Mare Island, California he interviewed crew members of British warships in for repairs and he went on shakedown cruises, and then was a passenger on an American warship on patrol in the Pacific. Many articles and stories resulted from his wartime naval contacts, but the single most important product of this relationship was his novel of praise to the Royal Navy, *The Ship* (1943), the story of a cruiser's single day of action in the Mediterranean Sea. Later on in the war, Forester's cruise on the United States Navy warship resulted in Forester's novel of the American Navy in convoy conflict: *The Good Shepherd* (1955).

Meanwhile, two more successful novels found their way to print, *The Earthly Paradise* (1940), published in the United States as *To the Indies,* a fictionalized account of Columbus's third voyage to America; and a Hornblower-type novel using an American captain during the war of 1812 as hero, *The Captain from Connecticut* (1941). During this period Forester began his long and profitable relationship with the most popular general magazine of its time, the *Saturday Evening Post.*

In the summer of 1943 Forester was struck down with an illness so serious that any person of less courage would most likely have damned his or her fate and given up on life. The illness struck at the very moment Forester was engaged in his happiest pursuit. The United States Navy had invited him to sail with the battleship U.S.S. *Tenessee,* under Admiral Thomas C. Kinkaid, flagship of the blockading squadron attacking Japanese installations on Kiska in the Aleutian Islands.[58] Forester was walking the *Tenessee's* quarterdeck with her captain when he began to experience excruciating pains in his legs. Each day they grew worse. Forester believed he was getting rheumatism from the cold and damp of the Bering Sea. He got back to sunny California as soon as he could, but the pain persisted until he was no longer able to walk more than a few yards. Finally he went to a physician and then to specialists. The diagnosis was arteriosclerosis. He was doomed to be a limping cripple, able to walk only a few yards without resting and severe pain, forced to live for the rest of his life with the fear of amputation of one or both legs.

Forester stopped writing briefly. The Anglo-American naval novel he had plotted out was put off. Years later he would go back and it would come to life as *The Good Shepherd.* Meanwhile depression gripped him. It was Hornblower who saved Forester. The author found that he could more easily lose himself in a Hornblower tale with the settings and time now so familiar, than in any other story.

Hornblower also provided Forester the opportunity to go to sea again. The growing popularity of the novels caused the British Admiralty and the United States Navy Department to compete with each other to get the popular sea writer aboard their ships. A navy car would call for him at his home in Berkeley and take him to the accommodation ladder of a large warship at the San Francisco Navy Yard; a little help up, and through the gangway, a few steps to the wardroom and an officer's compartment, and Forester, bad legs and all, was safely stowed aboard. The navy showed Forester that his loss of personal mobility did not mean that he had to be a total invalid. Forester soon realized that "even though I could only walk a few yards, I could still go to sea. It is never more than a few yards from a wardroom to a bridge, and although I would never again walk a quarter-deck, I could still feel the heave of the deck under my feet or look down at the bows crashing through the rollers."[59]

Now Forester eschewed solitude more than ever. He wished to be with people. He went to parties and let people dote on him. He actually began to increase his travel. Most important of all, "Doctor Hornblower"[60] demanded more life, more adventure. If his writer was indeed "living on borrowed time," then he had better get him to work, and he did. Back went Forester to 1,000 words a day, and *The Commodore* (1945), published in America as *Commodore Hornblower,* was on the way.

Forester's ability to work was severely limited during the remaining twenty-three years of his life, but he was happy once more. He kept his weight down to a lean, wiry, almost emaciated-looking 135 pounds (he was six feet tall), and when help was needed there simply was not a lot of bulk to shift. What a novelist needs is a creative, flexible, focusing mind and this Forester had almost until the end, regardless of the condition of his body. Even a heart attack in 1948 did not appreciably slow his literary output or his enjoyment of life.

In 1944 Cecil and Kathleen were divorced. In 1947 Forester mar-

ried Dorothy Ellen Foster, daughter of a shipping magnate, a woman
he had first met during a tennis tournament in London in 1921. She
was a demure, gentle woman about his own age; they were well-suited
and remained together happily for the rest of his life.
While writing *Lord Hornblower* (1946) the Royal Navy flew him to
the Pacific and placed him aboard H.M.S. *Swiftsure*, a cruiser. The
last words of *Lord Hornblower* were written after V-J day on the ship
when the duty marine had brought him his morning cup of tea, as
Hornblower's steward might have served a first cup of coffee, and
Forester had retired to his writing space:

Inside the thin shield protecting a four-poster pom-pom I was exposed to the
early sun and sheltered from the early wind and interrupters. Steadily my pen
filled the sheet and those long-thought-out last words came nearer and nearer.
I heard the measured tramp of the marines on the quarterdeck I heard sharp
orders given, and the band break into its lively march. The last sentence was
half finished when the pipes of the bos'n's mates called everyone to attention.
"General salute! Pr'ent arms!" bellowed the marine subaltern. The band
played God Save the King, and everyone stood at attention as the white ensign
rose over Tokyo Bay. God Save the King ended and The Star Spangled Banner
began, and with the "home of the brave," the pipes put us at ease. "Slo-o-ope
arms!" bellowed the subaltern, and I sat down and wrote the last six words.
Then I stood up; the white ensign was fluttering over Tokyo Bay, and
Mount Fujiyama was catching the sun in the distance. It was the last scene in
a long series, for Hornblower had been originally thought of while tossing in a
storm off the Azores in mid-Atlantic more than nine years before—the day
news came that Hitler's army had marched into the Rhineland. In a clairvoy-
ant moment, then, I had guessed at the dangers and perils to which England
would be submitted, and had made up my mind to write about her when, in
the old days, she had fought with her back to the wall and sea power had saved
her. And here I had written the last words of the long story while the white ensign told the last of Hitler's allies how long was the arm of sea power. Then I
realized I was hungry, and went down to the wardroom for breakfast.[61]

VIII   *Exploring New Territory*

Forester thought he had written out the project he had set for
himself, to relate in the days of Hitler how Britain had weathered
a similar crisis, equally disastrous, in the days of Napoleon, through
the courage and fortitude of her fighting men. However, Hornblower
was not finished with Forester and soon the author was filling in
the sailor's early years. *Mr. Midshipman Hornblower* appeared in
1950, *Lieutenant Hornblower* in 1952, and *Hornblower and the Atro-*

pos in 1953. In this period Forester wrote two of his most serious novels, neither one of which has anything to do with the sea: *The Sky and the Forest* (1948), a story of tribal warfare and colonialism in the Congo of the nineteenth century, and *Randall and the River of Time* (1950), which depicts the plight and victimization of a young English soldier during and immediately after World War I. This book is Forester's most philosophical work, exploring as it does the effects of chance on human destiny. Forester's post-World War II work was the most creative, fertile, and innovative in his forty-two-year career as a writer.

Forester's life settled into a three-faceted existence. First there was his daily writing, 1,000 or more words each day on two, perhaps three pages of yellow foolscap. Then there was the routine of the rest of his day with his wife, Dorothy, in their comfortable Berkeley home, obsessive reading of seven to ten books per week, going for long drives, playing twelfth-century music on his recorder, bridge games, and movies.[62] Lastly, incessant travel: constant journeys by ship or plane to Europe, Japan, and elsewhere, about which he "enjoyed discoursing with humor."[63] Forester and Dorothy even chartered a seventy foot schooner to sail the Pacific in the summer of 1958. Forester's semiinvalid condition simply did not stop his and Dorothy's constant tripping.[64]

On May 7, 1953, the British government apparently asked if he would be willing to accept honors from the Queen, perhaps the rank of Commander of the British Empire, or it could have been a lesser honor like the Order of the British Empire. He declined, stating he did not deserve the honor, but it is possible that he felt that he deserved more.

Long years after he had sailed with the American Navy, Forester wrote his story of the convoy war in the North Atlantic, with a World War II American naval officer as protagonist, *The Good Shepherd* (1955). Forester followed this work with his most serious history, a product of years of research,*The Age of Fighting Sail: The Story of the Naval War of 1812* (1956), published in England as *The Navy War of 1812*. This work became the most authoritative study of the naval actions of the second American war with Great Britain. In it Forester successfully challenged the claims made by American naval historians like Theodore Roosevelt that the War of 1812 ended in victory for the United States because of successful single ship actions.

A semihistory is Forester's *Hunting the Bismarck* (1959), published in America as *The Last Nine Days of the Bismarck*. Forester fictionalized the account of the German pocket battleship's last cruise and demise by putting undocumented words into the mouths of the participants in the naval campaign, but nevertheless it is both good history and good reading. Three more Hornblower novels emerged from the last years of Forester's work: *Hornblower in the West Indies* (1958), published in America as *Admiral Hornblower in the West Indies; Hornblower and the Hotspur* (1962); and the unfinished *Hornblower and the Crisis* (1967).

IX   *Last Work*

The last complete work of Forester's life was the delightful *Hornblower Companion* (1964). This work contains two parts, thirty maps (Forester should really have called them charts) of the locales of the Hornblower stories, and some eighty-five pages of notes on how, when, and why Forester came to write the various novels in the Hornblower series, as well as Forester's comments on his own writing methodology.

He had to work under publishers' deadlines for motivation. Plot was initially most important for him as he felt generally unable to develop characterization until the storyline was logically and fully set out. When all preparations were made, he simply began to write from page one onward:

> For there is no other way of writing a novel than to begin at the beginning and to continue to the end, and that is not quite the statement of the obvious as it might appear. Other people have other methods; I have heard of novels started in the middle, at the end, written in patches to be joined together later, but I have never felt the slightest desire to do this. The end is in my mind, of course, and so are the intermediate passages, and I rush forward, leaping from one solid foothold to the next, like Eliza leaping from one cake of ice to the next on the Ohio River.
>
> There is still need to think and plan, but on a different scale, and along different lines. The work is with me when I wake up in the morning; it is with me while I eat my breakfast in bed and run through the newspaper, while I shave and bathe and dress.[65]

According to Dorothy Forester and C. S. Forester's nephew, Stephen Troughton-Smith, the author preferred working facing a blank wall in order to invision scenes and then record with words. Novels or other books took three or four months of writing and involved intense concentration. As far as daily life was concerned, Forester "might as well have been under an anesthetic."[66] Initially, he would feel a distaste for his work and a belief that friends and critics who praised his efforts simply did not know what they were talking about, but after a while, like a father with a newborn child, he would begin to think "it a very wonderful baby indeed."[67]

In 1961 Forester suffered another severe heart attack. He was rushed to the hospital and given only an even chance to survive. His will to live did not fail him, nor was Hornblower ready to be committed to the sea and eternal rest. Forester went back to work to fill in the last of the early years of the Hornblower story including the officer's marriage in *Hornblower and the Hotspur* (1962). Work and nursing his health were the two poles of Forester's existence. His circulation was poor. He lay flat on his back much of the time and dictated often to a secretary rather than writing himself. Slowly but surely he recovered from the heart attack, or seemed to. He even made another trip around the world after finishing *Hornblower and the Hotspur*.[68]

Once more, after completing *The Hornblower Companion* on March 2, 1963, he stated that he was finished with the old sailor.[69] Another long trip followed, but a postscript written on March 5, 1964, indicated that he was back to work on a Hornblower novel, what would be the unfinished *Hornblower and the Crisis* (1967).

Forester was living too fast and working too hard for his weakened heart. Inevitably he suffered a severe stroke, in September 1964, and all activity came to an end. From then on the tired fighter merely lingered on in paralysis until his heart gave out on April 2, 1966. He had almost lived long enough to complete the Hornblower Saga, if indeed it ever would have been finished.

Writing in his early thirties Forester had said that

. . . the time will come when I am an old man, a nuisance to my children and a burden upon my wife, maundering in senility towards a grave which I alone will not regard as a merciful release. And when I die there may be a paragraph or two in the newspapers, and a few people yet unborn reading them will say to themselves. "C.S. Forester? Oh, yes, I've read one or two of his novels," and turn to the sporting page. After that my name will linger in the British Museum Reading Room catalogue for a space at the head of a long list of books for which no one will ever ask.[70]

Not so, not so. Forester remains an extremely popular writer. The Hornblower books, particularly, gather new readers each year. Copies of a paperback series of the novels are widely available, and Forester is recognized as one of the masters of twentieth-century popular fiction. Only time will tell if the critics of the future will acknowledge a more profound contribution to literature by C. S. Forester.

CHAPTER 2

Apprenticeship and Early Writing: 1924–1931

FROM the beginning of his writing career, C. S. Forester was both historian and novelist. His heart was in the making of fiction and the biographies were hack work for him, but, in fact, his early novels were marred by improbable plots, poor structure, and inconsistent characters, while his biographies were thoroughly researched, consistently interesting, and cast in a dramatic mold. Forester's first memorable heroes and heroines were figures of history, not figments of his imagination. The early biographies, rather than the apprentice novels, were the training ground for the distinguished historical novels of Forester's maturity. The two travel books, commissioned by a generous publisher, provided some grist for the creative mill that eventually would produce one of Forester's finest novels: *The African Queen* (1935).

I *Early Novels*

The young Forester hurled himself into the novel form, writing an incredible 6,000 words a day in order to produce a first novel that was, in the author's own words, "atrociously bad."[1] After rejection by several publishers, Forester withdrew the book from consideration and never again tried to have it published. Before that decision, his writing fury still up, the young, would-be novelist had finished a second work, which would see print as his second published novel.

The Paid Piper (1942) was written without a plan, something Forester was never to do again. Working in a cheerless, unheated rented room, Forester simply put down imaginary episodes which he tried to link together by means of a storytelling framework. Years later the novelist would note, painfully, that the work is "episodic, somewhat incoherent . . . [and] a very bad book."[2] In the novel one Sir William Sydenham, a wealthy government official who has just returned to London from a long tour of duty in Cairo, sees a Cockney toy-seller peddling his wares one evening on the streets and, without apparent motivation, invites the supposedly impoverished vendor to his home for dinner and to provide amusement as a storyteller.

The Cockney, it soon turns out, is neither a Cockney nor a tramp, but is rather a middle-class young man who seems to be a kind of romanticized version of a hobo. He has had a good private-school education, he carries fifty gold sovereigns concealed on his person in case of emergency, and he spends his time visiting London and environs, earning a few shillings a day to keep alive on, reading, sunning, and even writing a novel; surely a hard-working young novelist's idealization of a tramp's life. Additionally, the tramp, Mr. Cardinal, as he calls himself, has impeccable table manners: "At table, his napkin over his knees, his manners were perfection, although he ate with evident appetite. He had some slight knowledge of Syrian and Persian antiques and we [Sir William and Mr. Cardinal] conversed easily on the subject. . . ."[3] Forester may have identified with the adventuring, storytelling hobo and the ex-Anglo-Egyptian official, Sir William, may have been an idealized portrait of his father.

The Paid Piper contains some fourteen stories, each resulting from a visit to Sir William by Mr. Cardinal. Most of the time Cardinal is the storyteller, but the butler, Higgins, is also recruited as a contributor to the Decameron or Canterbury Tales situation, and even Sir William contributes a tale. There is a ghost story, and a ghost ape story, a suicide tale, a revenge of a servant against his master for the death of the servant's betrayed sister, and a man who goes mad seeking the perfect life. Sir William offers a humorous story explaining how he won the Order of the Red Dragon of the Kingdom of Mondania while serving in Egypt. However, by far the most interesting and most outlandish tales are those offered by Cardinal in which he recounts his adventures in the Middle East. Starting out drunk in a gambling house in Suez, Cardinal finds that the beautiful wife of the villainous proprietor is madly in love with him. The husband, attempting to kill young Cardinal, is himself killed. The lovers flee across the Sinai and reach Damascus, where the hero first takes ill and then is imprisoned. He winds up in the

Turkish Army and finds himself facing the Allied Army at Gallipoli. He shoots his Turkish comrades and deserts to the British. The prison scenes and battle scenes are exquisitely and convincingly described by the young writer, who has seen neither battle nor the inside of a Syrian jail.

Despite the passionate circumstances of Cardinal's and his Sophie's flight, no sex is allowed to mar the tale. The hero travels as Sophie's servant because his Arabic is not good enough to allow him to pass as her husband.[4] They never do consummate their love affair to the great relief of the priggish Cardinal. Sophie may have been expected to find some solace in the fact that she is frequently manhandled by lascivious officials along the way, with most of the action taking place off stage and merely hinted at.

Higgins most appetizing contribution to an evening's activities is the story of two lovers caught by the madly jealous husband. Shades of Edgar Allan Poe's "The Cask of the Amantillado": the husband walls up the lovers in the cellar until finally the starving man goes mad and eats his dead lover.

Some of the dialogue in the book is atrocious. Witness Sophie's realization that she and Cardinal must leave Suez: " 'Oh, my hero!' " she said! 'We must depart at once.' "[5] When Sir William takes to his bed because of an injury, Cardinal reacts thusly: " 'This is bad luck,' he said as he sat down. 'Dislocated knees are a tiresome business.' "[6]

Late in the book the reader learns that Cardinal has written a fairly successful novel. His description of his efforts as a novelist are clearly an account of Forester's first try:

It was winter-time, and I was hard up. A bright idea struck me. Why not write that novel and bring in some much wanted cash? I spent one of my few remaining half-crowns on a supply of foolscap, and started in. . . . I found (I believe it is the usual experience) that I could write a thousand words an hour. The novel would be 65,000 words long. Splendid! Nine days' really hard work would finish the thing off. My first day I actually completed my quota of seven thousand words, and was in an ecstasy. True, I earned no money that day, but that was a minor detail. But I soon found that I had to pay for such a debauch. I had started at ten in the morning; I ended at eight at night, and only when I rose from the table did I realise what a fool I had been. My hand ached with writing, my head ached with thinking, and the rest of me ached with sitting. I was abominably hungry, and at the same time I felt too tired to eat. Novel writing is far and away the most exhausting work I know.[7]

Cardinal hates publishers. They exploit young writers and that is the reason he will never write another novel. The tramp goes into great detail describing his unpleasant and unfortunate relationship with the publisher of his book, who says:

"This—er—this manuscript of yours," he went on, "it seems quite good in places. Of course, it's very amateurish, and obvious first novel, you know, and of course it's very tame in certain passages, but still, there's something about it. I expect we shall lose money over it, but for all that, we want to do you a good turn, and we'll publish it. . . ."
"Now about terms," began the publisher, with narrowing eyes. "Of course you would prefer royalty terms, since you have such supreme confidence in your book."
I nodded.
"Shall we say five per cent royalty?" he said, "at seven-and six a volume, that means about fivepence each for you. Perhaps twenty pounds altogether six months after publication. That's very good pay, you know. That's better terms than you'd have anywhere else."
I looked my unbelief at him, and he exploded about the bad times there were in the publishing world and how even worse ones were coming, and how there was a glut of novels in the market.
"You're being exceptionally well treated, . . ." he wound up.[8]

Forester, if not Cardinal, will mellow in his attitude toward publishers with the passing of time, but when he was writing *The Paid Piper* he clearly felt that publishers were his mortal enemies. Consequently, the most realistic and best written passages of the book are those in the chapter entitled "Not Hereafter" which deal with the beginning writer's problems in the post/World War I London world of publishing.

Also autobiographical in this book is Forester's reference to medical-school procedures, as when Cardinal's dying friend Ikey begs him: " 'Bury me decently, won't you. . .' he said. 'You know what will 'appen if you don't. Little knives going to an' fro an' young men laughing over my body.' "[9] The dissecting room was not far behind Forester or long out of his thoughts.

The best of this first novel to be accepted for publication is the fine characterization of Cardinal. The picaresque hero of Middle Eastern adventures, the reluctant lover, the happy tramp by choice, the clever François Villon of the streets of London, is a delightful character who evidences Forester's talent and potential as a writer with skills in depicting romantic heroes in exotic settings.

A *Pawn among Kings* (1924) was the third written and first published book of that desperate half year of young Forester's attack on
the novel. From boyhood on, Forester was fascinated by the life
and career of Napoleon. Even in *The Paid Piper*, when he wished
to coin an adverbial expression indicating grandeur or opulence, he
wrote: "Tramps can live Napoleonically on the countryside. . . ."[10]
The great Frenchman would soon be the subject for Forester's first
biography, *Napoleon and His Court* (1924), the book he would write
after *A Pawn among Kings*, and then Napoleon would develop into
the great adversary in Forester's work, the villain behind French
aggression in *Death to the French* (1932), *The Gun* (1933), and of
course, the Hornblower epic.

Recalling his extensive knowledge of Napoleon's career, Forester
remembered three times in the emperor's campaigns when he hes-
itated or delayed to his great cost: in 1812 at Moscow, in 1813 after
the battle of Dresden when he failed to follow and annihilate the
retreating Austrians, and during the Waterloo campaign in 1815
when he neglected to press the Prussian army and lost the advantage
that might have brought him victory at Waterloo. Forester decided
that he could write an historical novel in which a mythical mistress,
Mademoiselle Marie de Berzeny, a beautiful seventeen-year-old
Hungarian girl sent to him by a lifelong enemy from Corsica and
youth, Count Andrea Pozzo di Borgo, causes Napoleon to delay the
retreat from the Russian capital while he dallies in her arms. She
falls in love with the emperor, follows Napoleon, and is wounded
at the battle of Dresden while disguised as a member of his staff.
Of course, Napoleon tends to her rather than pursue the fleeing
enemy. Eventually they are separated by war, but she reappears
at Ligny, before Waterloo, and she shoots herself in Napoleon's tent
so that the emperor is delayed for some three or four critical hours
as he mourns for and buries his former love. Thus Napoleon's ruin-
ation and the downfall of the French are caused by love of one
woman. Now Forester could really let loose his imagination. Infantry
could march, wheel, and stand and fire. Artillery could thunder.
Cavalry could charge bravely into the guns. Forester "burned Moscow . . . just as five hundred novelists from Tolstoi to G. A. Henty
had done before. . . ."[11]

Improbable though the plot may be, *A Pawn among Kings* has
much in it to commend it. Although Napoleon remains a shadowy
figure and a cardboard cutout, and Marie seldom rises above the
level of a Victorian heroine who cannot love any other man once

she has had her first "lover" even though initially she hated the man, nevertheless the novel holds the reader's rapt attention by means of Forester's already considerable ability to write historical narrative, combined with the young writer's amazing depth of knowledge of Napoleonic history and lore. The chapter titled "Disaster" recreates the terrible retreat of the Grand Army from Moscow with fascinating verisimilitude within a powerful prose style that foreshadows the best descriptive work of the Hornblower Saga. Napoleon is better portrayed through his effect on others than by personal description:

The great captain was regarded with a terror which almost drove its victims mad, and the terror was hardly allayed by the doubts with which both soldiers and peoples regarded their leaders. Every general had at one time or another submitted to Napoleon; every monarch had implored his mercy. Not a regiment was awaiting his attack that had not had its laurels smirched in some lost battle against him; half the soldiers themselves had served under him. The allies awaited his attack as a bird awaits a snake, paralysed, trembling, terrified. And Marie awaited she knew not what, weary, fluttering, frightened.[12]

No wonder the publishers wanted Forester to write a biography of Napoleon and other lives of the Napoleonic period. By the same token, the publishers, who refused to take another novel by Forester, greedy though they were for his biographies, may have despaired for the young writer's ability to write fiction as they read of a heroine who, after rescue from a battlefield, is made to say by Forester:

"Oh, the bonny men," said Marie, "all dead and rotten, with their fingers poking through the earth and beckoning to me. Tee-hee. All dead, every one of them. Tee-hee-ee."[13]

Like Hornblower, Marie falls ill with typhus.[14] Unlike Hornblower or even Rifleman Dodd in *Death to the French* she never realistically blends into history. However, the future outstanding historical novelist is learning his craft.

C. S. Forester's first critically and commercially successful novel was also his first thriller novel. *Payment Deferred* (1926) made Forester's reputation as a novelist. It also spurred him into writing two other thrillers, neither of which was as skillfully written nor as well received as *Payment Deferred*, *The Wonderful Week* (1927) and

Plain Murder (1930). In each of these three books the protagonist is an ordinary man, a clerical type. The protagonist is also lower middle class, financially strapped, and married, except in *The Wonderful Week*, where the hero winds up married and financially strapped. All the plots are painstakingly worked out and improbabilities are few. In each case Forester is, however, more concerned with the psychology of the protagonist as sociological, emotional, economic, and other external forces are brought to bear on him, diverting and transmuting his careful plans for himself.

Payment Deferred is, as a critic in the *London Daily News* called it, "a striking study in suspense and terror." William Marble, the villainous protagonist, is a weak-moraled, cruel, alcoholic bank clerk, married to a frail, shabby woman named Annie. They have two children and more debts than they can pay. A nephew from Australia, James Medland, pays the family a surprise visit. The young man is an orphan, recently arrived and alone in England, and he possesses a considerable amount of cash, which Marble just happens to see. After sending his family off to bed, Marble plies Medland with whiskey and attempts to negotiate a loan. The young man quickly precludes such an outcome to the conversation. Marble decides to murder Medland for his money. He commits the perfect crime, poisoning the youth with potassium cyanide from his photography equipment and burying the body in the garden. From that moment on, Marble lives in constant terror, always afraid that the body will be discovered and he will hang. He feels he must buy the house and land he presently rents, but he does not have enough money. The money from Medland's wallet has been going to pay pressing bills and for whiskey. In desperation, he contrives a brilliant scheme to make a financial killing on foreign-exchange currency speculation with the pecuniary help of an affable bookmaker named Saunders. The scheme succeeds admirably and Marble is set for life.

He is not happy, however; his fear of detection remains unassuaged. Nor is his family happy, either. Annie Marble receives little satisfaction from her new clothes and new furniture. She does not understand why her husband will not allow her any household help and she must work harder than ever. Meanwhile Marble has acquired a predatory French mistress, Madame Collins, who eventually will blackmail him successfully. The children are taken from their local schools and put into more prestigious private institutions. The son John is patently unhappy. Only his love for his motorcycle and his pleasure in reading sustain him. Finally he drives home unexpectedly from a seaside vacation with his mother and sister, to find his father in the plump arms of Mrs. Collins. Aghast, John rushes from the house, speeds away on his motorcycle, and crashes to death against a high wall. (Forester had become interested in motorcycles as his fiancée, Kathleen Belcher, was a motorcycle enthusiast. He will kill off another young man on a motorcycle in *Plain Murder*.)

The daughter, Winnie, learns all the wrong things at school, grows to disdain her dowdy mother and drunken father, and eventually leaves home for good after a family argument. Annie Marble takes ill. Madame Collins, who has left her pliant English husband and run away to France, sends a letter to Will, demanding more money to prevent disclosure of their illicit affair. Annie accidentally reads the letter and is shocked into suicidal despair. Previously she had guessed about Medland and so she gets some of the potassium cyanide from her husband's photography shelf and poisons herself. Unfortunately for Marble, her suicide appears to be murder and so, years after he killed his nephew, Marble is executed for the crime of murdering his wife, a crime of which he is innocent. Payment for murder may have been deferred, but it is exacted after all.

William Marble is a brilliantly constructed character. Stimulated by all-devouring fear, he rises to the need to make a large sum of money quickly, with nerve, daring, courage, and intelligence and then sinks back into brutish torpor. He cannot escape the ironic end fate has in store for him, but the reader is fascinated by the wriggling creature on the hook of destiny. Mrs. Marble is almost equally well drawn. Her dark, pathetic, miserable, hopeless life evokes deep sympathy. Best of all, however, is the book's ability to hold the reader's attention. The suspense factor hinges on the juxtaposition of the reader's growing sense of the inevitability of Marble's downfall with wonder as to how Forester will have his villain get his just dessert. Ultimately, there is enough sympathy for a man who although "possessed of twenty-seven thousand pounds . . . spent his evening, as long as he was sober, sitting in a dreary little suburban drawing-room gazing out over a desolate suburban backyard, for fear lest some trespasser or some stray dog should find something out."[15] Despite the melodrama one cannot fault the *London Sunday Times* in naming *Payment Deferred* as one of the ninety-nine best crime stories. Forester would never equal this first effort in the mystery-thriller genre. Few English novels would match this book in suspense and only a masterpiece with metaphysical overtones like Graham Greene's *Brighton Rock* (1938) could surpass it.

The Wonderful Week (1927; American title: *A Wonderful Week*) is an entertaining tale that, unfortunately, is seriously marred in tone by several shifts from the comic and back again. The mystery-thriller format does not work well for Forester in the context of a plot which contains an excessive number of improbabilities. The hero is Harold Norman Atridge, a rather pathetic young London clerk, an orphan skimping by in a rooming-house existence on a minimum salary. Initially Forester presents him as a Walter Mitty type, making his humdrum life a little more bearable through day-dreaming. While being soundly trounced at tennis, his only recreation, Atridge fantasizes that he is an heroic colonel in Napoleon's cavalry:

His sword, his boots, the flanks of his horse, his very breeches were splashed and dripping with blood, but his sword arm continued to rise and fall with implacable ferocity and dazzling mechanical skill. A burly officer (in appearance singularly like Norton, the Singles Champion of the Morley Park Club), on a big black horse threw himself across the Colonel's path in a desperate attempt to check his career. But two quick feints on the Colonel's part left him helpless; for a fleeting second the officer saw his doom close upon him and his face was tortured into an expression of indescribable horror. Next instant the Colonel's blade was through his throat, and he fell from his saddle spluttering out his life in a scarlet torrent. Even that, thought Atridge, was hardly sufficient repayment for a 6–0 6–2 victory.[16]

Looking for an absent tennis partner, Atridge suddenly finds himself involved in the life of a pretty young thing named Marjorie Clarence, whose father is a delirious alcoholic and on his way to a sanitarium. Atridge helps Marjorie, the missing tennis partner, to subdue and commit the mad father, receiving for his pains a black eye from the father and Marjorie's determined assault on his bachelorhood, an assault which is successfully terminated by his acquiescence to marriage at the end of the book. This plot is sociologically interesting, depicting as it does the circumscribed life of lower middle class young people in London during the post–World War I period.

The plot turns incredible when Atridge, returning home on a Saturday night from a day of kissing Marjorie in the country and somewhat involuntarily getting further involved with her, witnesses a murder. He winds up with a packet of letters which turn out to

be, amazingly enough, the love letters of Prince Raphael of Lesser
Avaria which the ruler wrote to a Parisienne actress and which had
fallen into the hands of German industrialists trying to get business
concessions out of the government of Lesser Avaria. Atridge is shad-
owed by a villain described as having a "hawklike profile."[17] Unfortunately, Forester uses that element of caricature several times
in his early novels. "Hawklike profile" automatically means villain.
The simple and rather cowardly hero does not know what to do
with his find. He is kidnapped in the middle of the financial district
of London and whisked away to a tenement room where he is severely tortured. It is here that the clever lighthearted tone of the
book is demolished by the appearance of believable, sadistic villains
and the real pain Atridge feels. The book never recovers from this
tonal shift even though Forester tries to bring the original mood
back by having the hero escape by using his suspenders and mailing
the love letters to the British Foreign Secretary, who is able to call
off the various Avarian and German pursuers and arrange for Atridge
to receive a raise in salary so he can afford to marry Marjorie in the
end.

The phony kingdom, the slapstick chase, and the declining verisimilitude prevent the author from achieving what he apparently
set out to do: to write a witty psychological suspense novel that at
the same time offered a sociological observation of lower-middle-
class English contemporary urban life, the type of novel Evelyn
Waugh wrote so well. The fastidious and somewhat prissy hero is
well described and his character firmly established early in the book:

> Perhaps now it is obvious whence came the assortment of habits which
> endeared the grown-up Harold to his landlady. They were grained into him
> so deeply that before he was twelve Harold would sooner have eaten beetles
> in his porridge than eat it unpunctually, or with dirty hands, or while
> wearing bedroom slippers. To Harold "playing in the streets," which for
> a brief period seemed (as he contemplated it), more joyful than harp-playing
> in heaven, now appeared something too vile even to contemplate.[18]

The description of Atridge's rigid upbringing was drawn from the
author's own experience and perhaps because of a sense of too
personal identification with the protagonist, Forester turned to the
fantastic and improbable in his story. At the end he projects Atridge's
future life after all has settled down. Then "his unoccupied thoughts
will drift back to Napoleon, to Austerlitz. . . ."[19] The young Harold

Atridge, however, is clever enough to see the fault in his own story and to criticize, in a way, the happenings of the one mad week of his life: "Harold still sat with a mouthful of half-chewed beef. To be worried and anxious about a little broken china . . . when he had a king's love letters under his shirt and half-a-dozen men with revolvers waiting for him in the street and when less than twenty-four hours ago he had been the eyewitness of a brutal murder, showed a lack of sense of proportion. . . ."[20]

Forester's third and last suspense thriller, *Plain Murder* (1930), was more an attempt to follow up the success of *Payment Deferred* than was *The Wonderful Week*. In it, two clerks who work in an advertising firm murder their immediate superior because he has learned of their bribe-taking and plans to inform the company's owner and obtain their dismissal. The chief villain, expert plotter, and actual killer is Charles Morris, who is finely described by Forester as: "what a catholic taste might term a fine figure of a man— big and burly in his big overcoat, with plenty of colour in his dark, rather fleshy cheeks. His large nose was a little hooked; his thick lips were red and mobile; his dark eyes were intelligent but sly. The force of his personality was indubitable, he was clearly a man of energy and courage. But no cautious man would say it was an honest face; there was shiftiness to be read there, unscrupulousness, perhaps, and there was in no way any indication of intellect."[21]

Morris murders another employee of the firm who was an accessory to the original murder and who shows signs of cracking. He plans the second murder alone and is equally successful. The young clerk, Reddy, is dispatched by Morris's secretly disabling his "friend's" motorcycle so that Reddy crashes at the bottom of a hill. Forester, perhaps thanks to his wife's interest, is quite knowledgeable about motorcycles at this time.

Flushed with success, the conscience-less Morris then plans to murder his accomplice Oldroyd and his own wife, with the intention of marrying the boss's daughter. He fails at these and is himself killed by Oldroyd, who suddenly turns into a rather clever person in the very last chapter of the book, whereas he was portrayed as a clod until that point. Thus in the end, either for the sake of poetic justice or because he had written himself into a corner in which a clever murderer was surely to escape punishment, Forester damages both the main characterizations in the novel, Morris and Oldroyd, by suddenly stripping the former of his intelligence and then endowing the latter with that attribute. Now Oldroyd will escape punishment presumedly because he had become the instrument of fate or divine judgment. Up to the last chapter, however, "the fierce resolution and stern determination which [Morris] displayed were comparably those of a Drake or Wellington."[22] The born criminal has his best moments inspired by the intense experience of murder as with William Marble. With Morris, Forester again attempts to show the effects of a first crime on the mind of an intelligent but otherwise ordinary man, whose most profound moment in life is the planning for and committing of the crime. The end of *Plain Murder*, unlike that of the far superior *Payment Deferred*, lets the reader down. Neither Morris as villain nor Forester as novelist lives up to the expectation of consistency and credibility. Perhaps in realization of this failure, Forester wrote no more suspense thrillers.

Love Lies Dreaming (1927) followed *Payment Deferred* in order of writing and publishing. It is a toss-up as to whether this novel or *The Shadow of the Hawk* (1928) is Forester's weakest novel. He seems to have felt a requirement to write some fiction at the time he wrote *Love Lies Dreaming* and in a dry period turned to young married life, surely his own, for a subject. It was one which he was too close to to do anything with except string together some precious anecdotes in a vain attempt to come up with some structure akin to a plot.

The story concerns a twenty-seven-year-old novelist who has had a few novels published to date and has been married four years. The marriage, an upper-middle-class one, is extremely genteel. Structurally, the main crisis of the book centers on the young couple's inability to fire a seemingly inept, but actually hard-working and good-hearted cleaning lady. The book is as episodal as *The Paid Piper*. Dances, parties, tennis, and bridge games form the background for the actions of the novel. Also a touch of tragedy is worked in because the couple have suffered the birth of a stillborn infant. The most loving passage of the book is the protagonist's remembering the funeral of the infant:

For I had to arrange with a ghoulish man, hard of eye and oily of mouth, about Baby John's first and last ride through London streets. Baby John and I, alone in a carriage together, while Constance struggled back to health in that disinfectant-scented room at "The Laurels." Baby John and I, while the errand boys snatched off their cap as we passed, and the horses reined up to let us through—such of them as had drivers of any courtesy. Baby John and I; and he would never, much as I had looked forward to it, point wonderingly at the horses and the big, red omnibuses, never dribble excitedly at the pageant of the streets, never, never, never. February, and we passed half a dozen trees glorious in almond blossom, mocking the hopes I had built upon so slight a foundation. But with Baby John there rode fresh spring flowers, scented and wonderful. That was why Mrs. Rundle had asked for that advance payment of wages. A drunken husband left her no money at mid-week for flowers for Baby John.[23]

Forester may have meant the novel to be a compliment to his young wife, Kathleen. If so, he failed in that respect, for the wife in the book, Constance, is extremely vain, peevish, flirtatious, and selfish. She is given to locking her husband out of the bedroom when she is unhappy with him. He, in turn, babies and manipulates his wife. Sex and denial of sex are used, mostly by Constance, for reward and punishment.

Autobiographical elements abound in the book. The novelist hero is named Cecil, we finally learn on the last page. When he tries to steel himself on the issue of firing the housekeeper he says to himself: "Why the devil should you give way? It's not Napoleonic."[24] The fictionalized writer meets a quota of three pages of typescript per day, just about the way Forester wrote.[25] The couple plan a motorboat tour of the French rivers, a tour the Foresters would make and one Forester would write about in *The Voyage of the "Annie Marble"* (1929). Instead of using traditional endearments like "dear" and "darling," Cecil and Constance go around calling each other "Old Thing" as Cecil and Katherine would do later on on their motor boat, *Annie Marble*.

The most interesting aspect of *Love Lies Dreaming* is the depiction of upper-middle-class young married life in London between the wars. The built-in suspicion and antagonism between the sexes is disconcerting. The snobbery and class rigidity are less surprising. A reader living in the last quarter of the twentieth century might be given to surmise that the world of Noel Coward comedy really did exist at one time.

It does not seem possible that Forester planned *The Shadow of the Hawk* (1928; American title: *The Daughter of the Hawk*) at all before beginning to write. It was his tenth published book in four years and clearly he was writing too much and too fast. The novel seems to be two separate works. The first is a story about an English planter in a South American state called the Rainless Republic. Major Francis John Rolfe returns to his adopted Latin American country after service in the British Army during World War I only to find that his property has been stolen by a new dictator and he is *persona non grata*. Infuriated, he mounts a guerrilla revolution with the aid of his English sidekick, Henry Dawkins, a physical giant. The revolt is temporarily successful but soon the superior firepower of the enemy prevails. Major Rolfe is killed and Dawkins is sent to a hellish prison island on a life sentence of hard labor. The description of the military campaign is fascinating. The terror of Bird's Island is very real for the reader. Forester describes the prison revolt masterfully:

. . . all the prisoners came rushing out, tearing themselves fearfully on stray strands of barbed wire, trampling underfoot those who fell, and proclaiming, by their wild yells, to the opposed companies of infantry that two hundred maddened criminals were let loose on their flank. Some of the startled soldiers fired wildly into the dark mass of men as it came surging out in the moonlight, but the surprise was too great to be withstood. Both the long thin firing lines crumpled up and drifted away across the island, still firing at each other, at the escaped prisoners, and of course, in their panic, at themselves, while the prisoners, masterless and leaderless, broke up into a swarm of raging madmen scattering hither and thither, some making blindly for the sea, some racing for the stores of food and drink in the sheds behind the soldiers' huts, while a few blundered upon the adobe walled compound of the female prisoners—and stayed there. The whole island was soon dotted with men, armed and unarmed, in ones and twos, firing wildly at whomever came near, grappling in the half-light and fighting to the death with whomever they met, killing, fleeing, plundering, to the accompaniment of the flame and crackle of the rifle-fire and the eternal thunder of the surf. [26]

Dawkins escapes with a treasure and makes his way back to England a rich man. Up to this point the book is engrossing. The reader expects the serious political vein to continue, with Dawkins using his money to revenge the death of his old comrade in arms and liberate the Rainless Republic. The situation and the setting are not dissimilar to those in Joseph Conrad's *Nostromo* (1904), in which the earlier author also creates a fictitious Latin American Republic, Costaguana, for the novel's background. John Masefield also created a South American nation, Santa Barbara, suffering under a dictatorship and rescued with the help of Englishmen, in three novels: *Sard Harker* (1924), *ODTAA* (1926), and *The Taking of the ˙Gry* (1934). Since Forester alludes to an incident in Masefield's Latin American novels in *Long Before Forty*, it is possible that he read

Sard Harker and *ODTAA* before writing *The Shadow of the Hawk* and fashioned the Rainless Republic after Santa Barbara.[27] However, the exciting political novel ends with Dawkins's return to England and another story begins mid-book. Dawkins sets out to locate the daughter of his friend Rolfe, who had been left behind in England with her grandmother years ago, Rolfe's wife having died. Dawkins finds the ten-year-old Nina and decides to adopt her. The rest of the book deals with his growing paternal love for Nina and her growing filial devotion. Two major episodes ensue. In one, Dawkins and Nina take an exciting trip up an English river. In the other, Nina foils the designs on Dawkins attempted by an attractive widow, Mrs. Gateson-Slaughter. War, politics, justice, and the Rainless Republic are all completely forgotten by Dawkins as he learns golf, joins a good club, establishes an estate, all for the purpose of providing Nina with an affluent and privileged upbringing. Eventually she calls Dawkins "Daddy," to his delight.[28] At the end of the novel Nina has become a young lady in her late teens and unbelievably, indeed grotesquely, the seemingly asexual Dawkins, a man in his fifties, presumably, falls in love with her and Forester finishes this imperfect work with the hint that Nina and Hawkins might marry later on.

Even generally friendly reviewers were taken aback by *The Shadow of the Hawk*. The *London Daily News*, in typically British understatement, called the book "uneven" and the *London Daily Telegraph* noted that "the first and second halves . . . are wildly different." It is difficult to believe that Forester was living up to his own rule concerning the careful outlining and plotting of a novel. Additionally, Forester was still prone to occasional painful overwriting, as in this description of a wine: "It was the finest Burgundy the best wine merchant in Gilding could supply, and Mrs. Gateson-Slaughter had aired it with infinite care. It bore within it all the wit of Voltaire, the effectiveness of Maupassant, the exuberance of Borotra, the art of Coquelin, the splendor of Versailles, and the placid joys of the Saône. It warmed and it delighted; it was a heady nectar."[29]

The Shadow of the Hawk could have been one of the best novels of Forester's early period if he had stuck to the serious theme he began with. The shift in tone, theme, and location destroyed credibility. He would not make this mistake again. In fact, his next novel would not only evidence a deeply thought out and executed conception but would remain consistent in tone throughout.

Brown on Resolution (1929; American title: *Singlehanded*) is Forester's first naval story and first mature work of historical fiction. It
is a novel worthy to be listed with *The General* and *The African
Queen*. More so than *Payment Deferred*, it marks the emergence
of a mature fictional prose artist. The *London Daily Telegraph* correctly noted its "epic quality."

The book begins with a wounded British seaman, Leading Seaman
Albert Brown, dying on Resolution Island in the Galapagos Archi-
pelago of the Central Pacific:

He was huddled in a cleft in the gray-brown lava of which that desolate
island is largely composed, on his back with his knees half drawn up in his
fevered delirium. Sometimes he would mumble a few meaningless words
and writhe feebly on to his side, only to fall back again a second later. He
was dressed in what had once been a sailor's suit of tropical white, but now
it was so soiled and stained and draggled, so torn and frayed, as literally
to be quite unrecognizable—it was now only a few thin, filthy rags feebly
held together. His face was swollen and distorted, as were his hands, being
quite covered with hideous lumps as a result of the poisoned bites of a
myriad of flies—a little cloud of which hung murderously over him as he
lay, combining with the shimmering reek of the sun-scorched rock almost
to hide him from view. His feet, too, although a few fragments of what were
once shoes still clung to them, were horribly swollen and bruised and cut.
They were more like sodden lumps of raw horseflesh than human feet.[30]

A flashback ensues to a time twenty-one years earlier when a
British naval officer, Lieut.-Commander R. E. S. Saville-Samarez,
RN, was taking a train from Greenwich to London. He meets a Miss
Agatha Brown, the spinster daughter of a Noncomformist green-
grocer. An older virgin like Rose Sayer in *The African Queen*, she
is ready for her first fling and so they have a five-day love affair in
a hotel: they part and never see each other again. She is pregnant
and naturally her father and brothers are furious. Agatha leaves
home. Fortunately she has some money at her command and she
sets up life as a widow in Camberwell, the London suburb of Forester's youth. It is her intention to send her son, Albert, to a fine
preparatory school and then to the Naval College, but she becomes
ill and dies. Albert must find work. After a brief stint as a clerk, he
decides to follow the career his mother had intended for him and
one he too desired, but because of his lack of education he must
join the navy as a seaman and hope to work his way up to commissioned status. Albert is clearly of good stock and is rapidly promoted

to Leading Seaman on his first ship, the old cruiser H.M.S. *Charybdis*. Forester obviously deplores a system in which class dictates educational opportunities and they dictate rank. It is the autumn of 1914 and Britain is at war with Germany. The *Charybdis* is sent to the Pacific to hunt for the German cruiser squadron loose among the vast British merchant fleet in the Orient. Forester's *Charybdis* bears the name and general proportions of an obsolete British cruiser of the same name, built in 1893, but armed with a main battery of six-inch guns as well as the 4.7-inch guns the author ascribes to her.[31] He downgrades her armament so that she is no match for the German cruiser *Ziethen*, an imaginary ship armed with 5.9-inch guns, which meets the *Charybdis* in the Pacific and destroys her in a brief but terrible battle.

Forester really comes into his own as a naval writer with his powerful descriptions of modern naval action foreshadowing superlative passages in such books as: *The Ship* (1943), *The Good Shepherd* (1955), and *Hunting the Bismarck* (1959). The fierce action between the two cruisers nears its inevitable end:

Even as *Charybdis* made her last hit her death was in the air. It smote her hard upon her injured side; it reached and detonated the starboard magazine so that a crashing explosion tore the ship across. The hungry sea boiled in; the stokers and the artificers and the engineers whom the explosion had not killed died in their scores as the water trapped them below decks. Even as the boilers exploded, even as the ship drove madly below the surface, *Ziethen's* last salvo smote her and burst amid the chaos caused by its predecessors. In thirty seconds *Charybdis* had passed from a living thing to a dead, from a fighting ship to a twisted tangle of iron falling through the sunlit waters of the Pacific down into the freezing darkness of the unfathomed bottom. Above her the circling whirlpools lived their scanty minute amid the vast bubbles which came boiling up to the surface; a smear of oil and coal dust marred the azure beauty of the Pacific, and its centre floated a little gathering of wreckage, human and inhuman, living and dead—nearly all dead.[32]

Brown is one of only three British survivors. He is rescued by the Germans. The *Ziethen* has received slight damage and her captain brings her to uninhabited Resolution Island to make repairs that should take no more than twenty-four hours. Brown, although not a deep-thinking person, is nevertheless very patriotic. His two British fellow prisoners are severely wounded and he is basically alone in a sea of enemies. Now Forester has his first chance to explore individual enterprise and action against overwhelming odds with the protagonist solely responsible for his own acts.

Brown steals a rifle and ammunition and escapes to the island, where he holds off the Germans and delays the repairs on the ship for an additional forty-eight hours. Finally he is shot and killed and the *Ziethen* is able to resume her cruise. However, the delay has allowed the British battle cruiser H. M. S. *Leopard*, another fictitious vessel, with twelve-inch guns, to hove into sight and destroy the *Ziethen*. There are no German survivors and so the world would never learn that it was the resolute action of one British seaman that made possible the destruction of the raider. Particularly, the captain of the *Leopard* will never know the truth. He is now Captain Richard E. S. Saville-Samarez, RN, CB, MVO. The main irony of the book thus is the fact that the unknown son has died to make the reputation of his unknown father. *Brown on Resolution* is indeed a well-planned and exquisitely plotted novel.

After Brown, Saville-Samarez is the most interesting character in the novel. Forester has entered into an antiwar, antiofficer period. His patriotism remains unshaken but he has come to think less of British leadership in World War I. This belief and lack of confidence will peak with the creation of General Curzon in *The General* (1936) and then disappear in Forester's fiction with World War II. Saville-Samarez is, not surprisingly, admired by Agatha at first sight: "and at first sight she knew him for what he was, a naval officer of the best brand of British stupidity. She liked his good clothes and his smooth cheeks . . . and they way he blushed when she caught him looking at her."[33] As a senior officer, Captain Saville-Samarez is brave but not bright, skilled but not creative, tactically competent but lacking in strategic foresightedness. He simply cannot see results beyond the immediately apparent:

Captain Saville-Samarez was not very different in appearance from what he had been twenty years before; he was not of the type that alters greatly with age. There were grey hairs now among his irrepressible brown ones, and authority and responsibility had brought character into his face; there were two firm vertical lines between his eyebrows, and his eyes seemed deeper set, and there was a grim line or two about his mouth, but he still seemed extraordinarily young, with his fresh complexion and upright carriage. Truth to tell, responsibility and authority sat lightly on his shoulders; he was never a man for deep thought or of much imagination, and the steadiness of his nerve had brought him out of whatever difficulties he had found himself in without any ageing flurry or worry. Little jobs like picking up moorings in a twenty-thousand-ton battleship in a crowded harbour with a full gale blowing he had simply accepted and carried through with automatically acquired skill, and without any frightening picture of what might happen if he made a mistake.[34]

One can only shudder at the thought that the system which promoted Saville-Samarez to captain will also raise him to flag rank and responsibility for tens of thousands of lives because of his tactical success over *Ziethen*. Thus in *Brown in Resolution*, Forester begins to deal with the political-military relationship which is the main theme of *The General*. Approaching the end of his apprentice and journeyman work as a novelist, Forester has begun to deal in ideas about courage, responsibility, the possibilities of action, and the meaning and ways of war as his world reached the halfway mark between two cataclysmic human disasters. War, Forester apparently believes at the time, consists of innumerable small actions of individual human beings, which ultimately determine victory or defeat despite the plans of great leaders. His viewpoint will change with Hornblower and World War II.

Although he used some of his research on the early Pacific naval battles of World War I in his next novel, *Two and Twenty* (1931), Forester reverted to autobiographical material to produce his last domestic novel of middle-class London Life between the wars. Like *Love Lies Dreaming*, *Two and Twenty* is lighthearted in tone and very thinly plotted. It could almost be a precursor to *Love Lies Dreaming*. The hero is Cecil M. Leigh, another hero with Forester's first name. Cecil is a destitute poet, twenty-two years old, of a very good family, son of a brave but dead general, living on his own having failed anatomy in medical school, and having alienated his relatives including his brilliant surgeon uncle.

At the onset of the novel, Cecil is so broke that he is boxing to earn a few pounds for food and lodging. He has learned to fight, as Forester did, by battling his way through the private-school system. The most exciting passages in the book, indeed the only action, are the first two chapters, dealing with Cecil's prizefighting. Like an upper-middle-class Rocky, Cecil defeats a more experienced and certainly better-fed opponent but breaks his hand in the process:

Never was it to be said of Leigh that he lost an opportunity. He sprang forward, hitting fiercely, rapidly, like some marvellous machine. A left-hand punch landed on Roger's stomach, so that he lurched feebly forward, dropping the guard which had automatically covered him up. Then a right-

hand punch, fierce and heavy as the one which had changed the fortunes
of the fight, reached his chin, and he fell, a tumbled, senseless heap.
Pandemonium broke loose in the theatre. The crowd yelled its glee at the
knockout, at the unexpected turning of the tables, at the piquant victory
of this bony unknown with the big nose. And Leigh stood by the ropes, not
very elated; and any elation he experience was discounted by the frightful
agony in his hand.[35]

Cecil must go to a hospital for physical therapy. At the same time
that a flashy but really meretricious epic poem of his, *Coronel*, based
on a famous World War I British naval defeat, is obtaining critical
recognition for him, he meets Miss Lucia Graves, senior student
at a physical-training college studying massage and apprenticing in
the hospital to which the poet is sent. She is a champion women's
field hockey player, as was Forester's first wife, and she is twenty-
one, beautiful, poised, well dressed, of a fine family, and determined
to marry the young poet. They marry secretly so that she can finish
school and receive her diploma. Cecil writes an equally successful
and ephemeral epic sequel to *Coronel*, entitled *The Falklands*, about
the subsequent British naval victory following the Battle of Coronel,
and is being hailed as perhaps the next poet laureate of England in
competition with John Masefield and Siegfried Sassoon. His family
is awed by this youth who gave up medicine but found fame on his
own. However, he realizes his limitations as a poet, even if the press
does not, and decides to return to medical school, from which he
will obviously graduate this time and wind up with a lucrative practice through the aid of his famous uncle. Lucia will practice her
profession of massage therapy at his side. Thus Cecil the fictitious
poet gives up his craft for the security and comfort of a medical
career, something which Cecil the real-life novelist would never
have dreamed of doing, or would he?

Forester was not wasting anything. He seems to have found a
place for the few leftover details of his personal life not already
included in *The Paid Piper* and *Love Lies Dreaming*. His somewhat
satiric depiction of the life of a young medical student is well done
and his description of the horrors of the dissecting room is hair-
raising.[36] However, there are lapses into inconsistency, inappro-
priateness, poor artistic judgment, and even bad taste, as, for example, when Forester has his hero plan and participate in a black
mass performed with a virgin corpse, and when he has his high-
minded poet visit a prostitute.

Forester may have had Cecil the poet give up literature and return to medicine because he was aware of the poor, forced quality of much of his early fiction. Forester must have realized that he needed to get himself directly out of his work, to become more objective, to give up justifying to family and world his decision to chose art over science, and to write books like *Brown on Resolution,* where he could best employ his ever growing knowledge of history and developing powers of narration.

II *Biographies*

Forester's work as a biographer paralleled his work as a novelist during the first eight years of his career as a professional writer. He came to biography not out of his deep love for history but out of his deep need for money. The publishers of the forthcoming *A Pawn among Kings* needed a book about Napoleon for their spring list and since the author of *A Pawn among Kings* obviously knew a great deal about the French emperor the commission was his.[37] His poverty would drive Forester to write four biographies which he later disowned and called hack work: *Napoleon and His Court* (1924), *Josephine: Napoleon's Empress* (1925), *Victor Emmanuel II and the Union of Italy* (1927), and *Louis XIV: King of France and Navarre* (1928), and one which he wrote "with real enthusiasm and with devoted hard work,"[38] *Nelson* (1929).

Regardless of his distaste for what he was doing, the massive commitment to biography forced Forester into patterns of writing requiring painstaking attention to details, research into primary sources, accuracy, and the pressing need to turn dry facts into living images. Forester never recognized the truth that the onerous labor of commissioned biography did far more to train him for the job of historical novelist than the innocuous and sometimes vacuous early novels like *The Paid Piper, Love Lies Dreaming, Shadow of the Hawk,* and *Two and Twenty.* Only *Payment Deferred, Plain Murder,* and *Brown on Resolution* show stylistic skills and general literary ability equal to the biographies, expecially *Victor Emmanuel II* and *Nelson.* *Payment Deferred* and *Plain Murder* on one side and *Brown on Resolution* on the other, represented two roads Forester could take as a novelist, one as a writer of crime thrillers and the other as an historical novelist. It was the training in historical biography that caused Forester to take the latter road, one which led to literary fame and financial success.

Napoleon and His Court marks the beginning of the long literary interest Forester evidenced for the great Frenchman. Significantly, Napoleon was a central figure in Forester's initial fiction and nonfiction, and even in lighthearted novels set in the contemporary time period references to Napoleon would creep in as if the emperor waited impatiently in the back of Forester's mind to be wheeled out like an old cannon in hope of use.

Writing *Napoleon and His Court*, Forester found he had a lot to say about the emperor and his family, courtiers, aides, and marshals. He was interested in Napoleon's personal relationships, in the daily contacts which in their own inevitable way contributed to the shaping of European history. Forester's first biographical prose is vigorous, imaginative, direct, and committed to the British prospective:

> There was only one nation in Europe which escaped the mesmerism of the man in the grey coat, and that was the British. It was only in Britain that they did not speak of him with bated breath as "the Emperor," and remained undaunted by his monstrous power and ruthless energy. To the English he was not His Imperial and Royal Majesty, Napoleon, Emperor of the French, King of Italy, Protector of the Confederation of the Rhine, and Mediator of the Helvetian Republic. No, the English thought of him merely as Boney, a fantastic figment of the imagination of the other people of the world, who were of course a queer lot with unaccountable fears and superstitions.
>
> But this Boney, this Corsican Ogre, incredible though he was, loomed appalingly large upon the horizon.[39]

Most of all, however, Forester is interested in the personality of Napoleon, more so than he was while writing *A Pawn among Kings,* where obstensively he had more of an opportunity to develop a character. It is voyeuristic history; it is history as gossip; in a sense it is not history at all if the concept of history is limited to great ideas or events; but *Napoleon and His Court* is always engrossing.

Forester explores Napoleon's relationship to women, again a parallel with *A Pawn among Kings,* and his relationship to the artists, performers, and writers of his day. Lastly, Forester indulged in an exercise he would often pursue. Chapter 16 is titled "What Might Have Been." In it, Forester rewrites the scenario of nineteenth-century European history based on alternative actions of Napoleon in regard to marriage, foreign policy, and personnel selection.

Forester realized that *Napoleon and His Court* was a better book than his first novels.[40] His publishers liked it too and they immediately commissioned another book on the Napoleonic period, *Josephine: Napoleon's Empress* (1925). Thus, three of Forester's first four published books dealt with Napoleon.

Josephine: Napoleon's Empress traces her life from her birth on the Island of Martinique in an impoverished background through her arranged marriage, the birth of her two children, the death of her first husband in the post-Revolutionary period, her life as the mistress of rich and powerful men, her meeting the twenty-six-year-old General Napoleon Bonaparte when she was thirty-two, his great passion for her, her marriage, her help in diplomacy, her extravagance, her life as a sad divorcée, her old age as a relic of the Napoleonic period, and her death. Forester almost treats Josephine as a fictional character as he finely draws a portrait of a poorly educated but clever woman who is generous with her friends and jealous over those she loved. Indeed, the book begins as if it were a work of fiction:

> The story reads at first rather like a child's fairy tale. At her christening, one might imagine, the good fairies and the bad were gathered together, quite in the regular style, and every time a good fairy made her a gift, a bad fairy balanced it in an evil fashion.
> "She will be beautiful," says one.
> "But she will outlive and regret her beauty," says another.
> "She will be a Queen, and more than a Queen."
> "And less as well."
> "Her husband will love her dearly."
> "But not for long."
> "She will have more jewels and pretty frocks than heart could wish for."
> "And she will always be in debt."
> "She will have loving children, who will rise to great positions."
> "But she will never have the child she longs for most."[41]

Josephine is further depicted as a survivor, one who rolls with the punches of fate and outlives her foes and her friends.

Forester selects the incident of Napoleon and Josephine's divorce as the great crisis and climax of her life. It is treated with consummate irony, for the divorce which Napoleon wanted in order to remarry and obtain the heir Josephine was unable to provide turned out to be Napoleon's disaster when his new father-in-law, the Emperor of Austria, betrays him, and the great Corsican is overthrown only nine years after the divorce he cajoled out of the empress. The same act, seemingly a disaster for poor Josephine, turns out to be her salvation, for it gained her sympathy and disassociated her from the emperor in enough time to allow her to survive the restoration of the Bourbon monarchy. The final irony for Forester was the fact that Napoleon's child by his new bride, Marie Louise of Austria, would provide no dynasty for him, while Josephine's grandson would be Napoleon III, Emperor of the French.

Forester's descriptions of the marriage of Napoleon and Josephine and their divorce are brilliant. The marriage ceremony receives a full measure of Forester's historical irony:

Napoleon had to wink to keep the holy oil out of his eyes—there was no arrangement in the Rubric for him to wipe it off with his pocket handkerchief—and how he tugged the crown out of the Pope's hands to place it himself on his own head, and then turned to Josephine and crowned her as well.

All things considered, everything went off very well. Something like two millions sterling had been spent; nobody concerned had anything to eat until after eight o'clock that night; Josephine lost the position conferred upon her in less than five years, and Napoleon lost his in less than nine. Lannes, for all the splendour of his present Colonel-General's uniform, was to die of gangrene four years hence, and Bessieres was to have his breast torn open by a cannon shot. Murat, who bore Josephine's crown on a cushion, and whose Gascon swagger was noticeable even when he was engaged upon such serious business, was to die at the hands of half a dozen unwashed Neapolitan police, against a wall in a little Calabrian town of which so far he had never heard. Pius, who prayed so solemnly that the most high and most august Emperor he was crowning would reign for ever, was soon to excommunicate that same Emperor, and was to suffer at the hands of his minions indignities innumerable. The soldiers who filled the streets were to perish of hunger, exposure, typhoid, dysentery, plague, while the citizens who cheered with them were to see Cossacks camped in their boulevards and the British infantry paraded upon the Place de l'Etoile.[42]

As the divorce is completed and the announcements made, the farewell moment between Napoleon and Josephine is recorded and the historical implications of the marriage recounted in such a manner as to indicate both Forester's growing interest in historical fiction and the beginning of Forester's two novels about the Peninsular War, *Death to the French* (1932) and *The Gun* (1933):

Napoleon took the precaution of having his secretary, Meneval, with him when he said goodbye to her, but not even his presence prevented a painful scene, Josephine fainted, and Napoleon handed her over to Meneval and hurried out of the room. When Josephine recovered, she passed down the halls; the thirty footmen in the ante-room sprang to life and rolled out the red carpet; the picket of Casseurs of the Guard came to attention; and the Empress-Queen-Dowager was assisted by her pages into her carriage and drove off.

Her life as Empress had been full of contradictions. While the constitution had allowed her no place therein the fiercest constitutional struggles of all that took place under the Empire had been waged about her position. The influence that many people believed her to have over the Emperor was non-existent. Yet her influence over international politics, wherein she was supposed to be only a cipher, was considerable. She had taken a leading part in the formation of the Confederation of the Rhine, and therefore it had been she who had raised the Bavarian battalions which had made possible the victories of Eckmuhl and Wagram, and therefore the annexation of the Austrian littoral and the close approach to perfection of the Continental System. The abdications at Bayonne had been largely her work. The Peninsular War had been brought about by her agency. It had been she, no less than Napoleon, who had sent Dupont forward to his destruction at Baylen, and who had sent the Red Lancers of the guard charging through the hail of grape from the batteries at the Somesierra. Perhaps some old stalwart of the line, crucified head downwards by maddened Spanish peasants, or some eighteen-year-old conscript shrieking in agony as the field-surgeons applied the hot irons to the stump of his leg, might have found some consolation in the fact that their sufferings were caused by the action of a lady. It is of course possible, but no one could call it probable.[43]

Seapower is not entirely neglected in *Josephine: Napoleon's Empress* despite its remoteness from the subject. The ever-tightening pressure of the British naval blockade and the significance of the Battle of Trafalgar are dealt with as Forester shows once more his mastery of the history of Europe in the Napoleonic period.

Josephine: Napoleon's Empress is more entertaining than *Napoleon and His Court*. At times it reads like tragedy. There is a distinct sense of drama behind it. A master storyteller is developing, one with the important ability to bring characters to life through combinations of fact and fiction juxtaposed against a moving background of historical events which seem to result not from the machinations of destiny nor from the inexorable and inevitable march of political and military events, but rather from the solecistic actions of the protagonists themselves.

Forester's in-depth knowledge of nineteenth-century history was not restricted to that of the Napoleonic period as his next book,

Victor Emmanuel II and the Union of Italy (1927), indicates. Forester, through his research, also mastered the intricacies of nineteenth-century Italian politics. Additionally, his lifelong study of military history stood him in good stead as he described with relish and accuracy the many battles which led to the ultimate unification of Italy in 1861. Most of all, Forester took a special interest in the character of Victor Emmanuel II, *Rè Galantuomo*, the honest king. In doing so he created a very interesting book that not only informs but also provides the suspense and involvement of an enjoyable novel.

The book begins with the disruption of the Italian States during the Napoleonic period[44] and the subsequent disastrous reign of Victor's father, Charles Albert, King of Sardinia. The work quickly focuses on Victor Emmanuel and the long and tortuous struggle for the unification of Italy against the desires of France, Prussia, Austria, and the Papacy. The relationship among Victor Emmanuel and the great Italian republican patriots, Giuseppe Garibaldi and Giuseppe Mazzini, is treated with delicate insight into the difficulties these strong men, committed to differing political ideologies but the same political goal, had with one another.

The influence of seapower, particularly British seapower, is again not neglected. Forester reminds the reader that: "All through the Napoleonic Wars Sicily had remained in Bourbon hands—even the straits of Messina were wide enough to keep back Napoleon . . . with the protection of a British fleet. . . ."[45]

However, it is the portrait of Victor Emmanuel II, from his birth in 1820, his youthful training as a soldier, his physical courage, his intelligence, his ability to break with the traditions and superstitions of the past, and his instinct for the middle path toward a desirable goal, an instinct that served him until his death in 1878, which overrides all political, military, economic, and social considerations in the book. Forester sums up the man delicately:

So everything depended upon the King, plain, simple, easy-going Victor Emmanuel, with his taste for chamois hunting in the Alps, and his little mercenary affairs with casual lights of love, and his domestic passion for his Rosina, and his liking for fried onions. Nothing flamboyant about him at all, no talk about "baptisms of fire," not even a stray telling phrase or two about "blood and iron," no international exhibitions, no white horse and glittering staff and appeals to "forty centuries," no tame buzzard trained to perch on his shoulder (to eat bacon out of his hat), only a mind as keen as a razor and an honesty as transparent as crystal.[46]

Louis XIV: King of France and Navarre (1928) is Forester's least effective and least interesting biography. It is more like a long encyclopedia article than a biography purporting to offer new and cogent ideas concerning the life and times of a great historical figure. Forester simply knew less and cared less about seventeenth-century European history than he did about nineteenth-century European events.

The book attempts to encapsule all aspects of the long life of the king who was born in 1638 and who reigned over one of France's most glorious periods, from 1643 to his death in 1715. Forester pays special attention to Louis's many military campaigns, to his several loves, to the elaborate court etiquette he devised to debilitate the nobility, and to the building of the great palace at Versailles, which Forester deplores: "Louis . . . had lavished upon Versailles the equivalent of two hundred dreadnaughts nowadays. In truth the French navy was like a cut flower, beautiful to look upon but doomed to early death."[47] Forester devotes an entire chapter, indeed the best in the book, to Louis's use or misuse of seapower. As if unable to escape from the nineteenth-century context, Forester makes continual comparisons of Louis with Napoleon[48] with the latter almost always the more admired. The biographer even compares Louis unfavorably to Victor Emmanuel II.[49] Lastly, Forester strainedly compares Napoleon's empress, Josephine, with Louis's mistress and second wife, Madame de Maintenon, based on the fact that both lived at one time in Martinique and both had arranged first marriages.[50]

The lukewarm biography is in part a result of Forester's limited respect and liking for Louis, whom he summarizes thusly:

. . . It seems necessary to decide that Louis was a man with too much care for himself, and, so, too little for others; with a passion for order which circumstances arising from his weaknesses prevented him from indulging to the full; of other likes and dislikes too moderate to be interesting; a very ordinary man in most respects, but above the average in diligence, industry, and in conscientiousness when he thought he ought to be conscientious. He was partial to flattery, though so dulled was his palate by it that it called for something fantastically spiced in the way of panegyric to move him. He was as good to his wife as she seemed to think he ought to be, and as good to his other women as he could be in accordance with his own whim and dignity. He was at his best as a king in court, a fair diplomat, a bad general, and a hopeless financier. He was a determined enemy and a good friend. . . . His reign bulks so large in the history of the world mainly because it occupies so large a part of it. He set several fashions which did no good, and he left a tradition which did harm. Yet, for all that, one cannot help liking him in an underhanded sort of fashion[51]

Forester's next and last biography was his happiest and most successful effort in the genre. *Nelson* (1929) represents the high water mark of Forester's work as a professional biographer working on consignment for a publisher. By emphasizing naval battles and the love affair between Admiral Lord Horatio Nelson and Lady Emma Hamilton, Forester shaped the dramatic material of Nelson's life in a manner to create the impact of historical fiction. The *Times Literary Supplement* succinctly noted: "The book is a contribution to literature rather than to history."

Nelson begins with a discussion of the primary documents, particularly the letters and documents, surviving from the admiral's time and relevant to his biography. Forester then relates Nelson's life in chronological order from his birth through his early career, his marriage, his several wounds, his long affair with Lady Emma, the four great Nelson battles: St. Vincent, The Nile, Copenhagen, and Trafalgar, and his death. More like a novel than a work of history, *Nelson* ends immediately upon the death of the hero with no afterwords concerning his influence on subsequent events of the Napoleonic campaigns, British naval policies in the later nineteenth century, or the denouement of Emma.

Forester first compares Nelson with Napoleon and to some extent with the Duke of Wellington, these men being the three gods in Forester's nineteenth-century Pantheon.[52] After establishing Nelson's different educational and class background as compared to both Napoleon and Wellington, Forester than proceeds to slowly and carefully depict the development of Britain's greatest naval leader. Forester, however, is always primarily interested in the man and not the action. He is fascinated by the *ménage à trois* relationship among the naval hero, his mistress, and her husband, the aged Sir William Hamilton. The strange trio are brilliantly described as if through the eyes of visitors:

They found there a very quiet gentleman in a black suit, toothless, yellow, shrunken, the very soul of hospitality and politeness, whom they had once known as the fiercest and most brilliant sailor in the whole navy. He deferred to a very tall woman, immensely stout, with a ravaged complexion, coarse in manner and beginning to be coarse in appearance, with a tendency to drink more champagne than was quite seemly, and whose one wish after leaving the dinner table was to settle down to cards. Somewhere in the background there was a vague shadow of a man, elegant of dress and deportment, despite the fact that his back was bent and his step tottering with years, who seemed to spend his time looking after the lady's lap-dogs and footstool, and who, if any one condescended to enter into conversation with him, would confess to a taste for quiet fishing which he unfortunately had little chance of indulging.[53]

Surely the most important aspect of Forester's research on Nelson and the writing of this, the best and the last of his biographies, is that Horatio Nelson is the unacknowledged prototype for Horatio Hornblower. The book *Nelson* provided Forester, beginning some seven years later, with at least twenty-seven incidents in the Hornblower Saga besides the obvious parallels of the heroes's first names, their middle-class origins, their love for independent commands, and their rapid rise in the service. The events in *Nelson* which Forester employs in the Saga of Hornblower include Nelson's marriage without love, his appointment to an income-producing sinecure as Colonel of Marines, his many inshore attacks on the French coast; the defecting of a French city from the Revolutionary cause; the eating of rats by hungry English naval officers and men; Nelson's becoming a Knight of the Bath and his wearing of the ribbon and the star of the order; Nelson's chronic seasickness; the loss of his arm and the medical procedures graphically described in the biography Forester transmutes from Nelson's arm to the leg of Hornblower's lieutenant, Bush; Nelson's youthful service on a guardship in the Medway; his falling in love with a woman above his station in life; his tutoring of a prince in naval affairs, his disregard for prize money; his arranging for his wife and his beloved to meet at dinner to the disadvantage of the former; Nelson's temporary appointment to the Sea Fencibles, a Coast Guard-type unit; his concern for the good mental and physical health of his command which led him to encourage theatricals and dancing on his ships; the towing of a storm-battered man-of-war off a dangerous coast by another warship; Nelson's capture of Spanish ships by boarding; transporting royalty and a full court on a warship; and a sojourn in France. *Nelson* even provided at least one important element of plot for Forester's *The Captain from Connecticut* (1941) in that both Nelson and the American Captain Peabody find employment for their brothers on their ships.

Thus the biography of Admiral Lord Nelson provided the vein

of character and incident which Forester would mine from 1936 to the end of his life for all his books dealing with fighting sail. In leaving history Forester could devote his artistic life to historical fiction, but the historian constantly existed and watched deep within the psyche of the creative writer.

III   *Travel Books*

Early in 1928, Forester, who must have been a most persuasive young man, persuaded his publisher to finance a motor-boat cruise through the waterways of France during the spring and summer of that year. The author, accompanied by his hockey-playing, motor-cycling, adventurous wife, set out in a fifteen-foot dinghy named *Annie Marble* after his wretched heroine in *Payment Deferred*, "a hardworking, unimaginative, obedient sort of creature who . . . possessed all the characteristics [Forester] should like to see in a boat. . . ."[54] The result of this trip, which took the Foresters from the mouth of the Seine to Rouen, Versailles (where Forester could reflect upon Louis XIV, whose biography he had just written), Paris, Fontainebleau, across via canals to the Loire and Orleans, Tours, Nantes, and the Bay of Biscay, was, as planned, the travel book *The Voyage of the "Annie Marble"* (1929).

The book is pleasant, chatty, witty and as leisurely written and easygoing as the boat trip itself. Forester describes his floating home as

. . . a punt-built dinghy. She is fifteen feet long, five feet wide at the widest point, which is one foot from the stern and her gunwale is nineteen inches high. With two people and luggage on board she draws four inches of water. Forward she is decked for a foot of her length making a locker which is useful as a depository for anything you will never possibly want. Floorboards rest upon her ribs, leaving a space beneath for any stray water on board. . . . Two canoe paddles will move her along at a speed reasonable enough in moderate currents. . . . The motor we used was an Evinrude Fastwin model, nominal H.P. 4.[55]

The Tatler described the book as "a joyous holiday" but there were problems along the way, particularly with the engine which Forester, not a mechanically oriented man who "could not tell a carburettor from a magnito,"[56] had much trouble with. It was a clutchless affair which required them to cast off into the current prior to starting, which the temperamental machine only occasionally did, until halfway through the cruise Forester learned how to adjust the needle valve.

The voyage and the writing of the book allowed the maturing writer to reflect humorously upon the life of a novelist:

> Novel writing wrecks homes. A man who writes for his living does not have to live anywhere in particular, and he could rarely afford to if he wanted to. The need to go and work every day in the same place keeps most people fairly stationary, but the novelist can earn his living, such as it is, wherever he happens to be. The effect is rather unsettling, just as easy divorce would be. A whim, a passing mood, readily induces him to move hearth and home elsewhere. He can accept invitations to live at other people's houses, and does so the more willingly because he can always plead work as an excuse to get him out of the clutches of bothersome hosts while his long-suffering wife is polite for the two of them.[57]

Three events recounted in *The Voyage of the "Annie Marble"* would have significance for Forester's later work. First Forester became intimately conversant with the life and ways of bargemen, information he would put to good use in *Hornblower and the Atropos* (1953). Second, a "great disaster" took place on the voyage: Forester ran the propeller into a bank by putting the engine accidentally in reverse.[58] It was ruined and Forester foolishly did not have a spare on board. Unlike Allnutt in *The African Queen*, he was unable to repair the prop and he had to dragoon his sister out from England to deliver a propeller to them in the middle of France. The incident fermented in the back of his mind and emerged as Allnutt's minor metallurgical miracle in the heart of Equatorial Africa, when Forester makes his half-educated boat engineer reforge a propeller on a primitive hearth as Forester must have wished he could have done for the *Annie Marble* and Kathleen in the heart of civilized France, waiting helplessly for the delivery. Last, Hornblower's magnificent escape from French authority by boating down the Loire to Nantes in *Flying Colours* (1938) is based on the knowledge of the river Forester acquired in the first voyage of the *Annie Marble* and set down in the book.

In the spring of 1929, because of the success of *The Voyage of the "Annie Marble,"* Forester's generous publishers sponsored a sequel voyage to write a sequel book, *The "Annie Marble" in Germany* (1930). The Foresters are more accomplished as cruising boatpeople now and the book, subsequently, has more of a "how to" flavor, particularly how to navigate the Elbe, Elde, Havel, and Oder rivers. More of the personal relations of the married adventurers emerge in this book and they continue to show their affection in true British fashion by calling each other "Old Thing." They motored over 1,000 miles, this time with another and more reliable engine, although they still had no clutch or auxiliary tank and Forester still had to cast off and hope. Now, however, he is able to change a broken shear pin, even if he still cannot forge a new prop.[59]

Forester could speak some German before the trip and his ability in that language improved dramatically on the voyage. By continually speaking with German World War I army and navy veterans he built up a store of knowledge which would serve him in good stead when he came to write such books as *The General* (1936), *Randall and the River of Time* (1950), and even *Hunting the Bismarck* (1959):

The gift was invaluable to me in Germany, because it made it possible for me to compare notes with the people I was most anxious to talk to. I met a man who was in the German Infantry of the Marine and who was wounded when the "Vindictive" came to Ostend; I met a man who served throughout the war in the famous 28th Grenadier division—the one which master-attacked at Cambrai in 1917, and which formed the spearhead of Ludendorff's attacks in the spring of 1918; I met men who had fought in battlecruisers, and others who had commanded Turkish warships; men who had fought in the Balkans, in the Ukraine, at Caporetto.[60]

Between 1924 and 1931 Forester served his apprenticeship and journeymanship to the writer's craft with hard work, publishing nine novels (discarding his first), five biographies, and two travel books. Often he wrote too fast and surely he wrote too much, at the cost of quality. His work had not made him famous or rich but *Payment Deferred* had brought him recognition. The efforts in biography, particularly the writing of *Nelson*, which he much enjoyed, steered him toward a compromise career. From now on most of his writing and surely his best work would be in the realm of historical fiction. The totalitarian villain of which Napoleon was the prototype until Hitler came to replace him in some of Forester's World War II work would remain locked in combat with an English hero, a Nelson surrogate, usually Hornblower, but sometimes a World War II naval officer, perhaps even an American, and once an ordinary rifleman named Dodd.

CHAPTER 3

The Historical Novelist Develops:
1932–1936

IN the 1930s C. S. Forester achieved his full maturity as a novelist. His production slowed down to a regular pace of one novel per year. Between 1932 and 1938 he published five individual novels, a little "how-to" book about turning one's home into a marionette theater, and the Captain Hornblower trilogy. Ultimately, Forester's critical reputation as a novelist is based on the production of this period, for in it he wrote his two finest novels, *The African Queen* (1935) and *The General* (1936), and he began the historical epic which would structure his future life as a novelist. In this period, Forester made some of his most profound observations of the English character under stress. He was able to begin to explore his interest in the ability of the individual human being, in command and, having full responsibility, to react to and deal with great stress and life or death decisions. It would all lead to the sea captain hero living in an historical period in which Forester was as much at home as he was in the twentieth century.

I *The Peninsular War Novels*

The Napoleonic wars had four major campaign areas: the plains of Middle Europe, where Napoleon defeated successive armies of Prussians, Austrians, Italians, and Russians in campaigns each of which seemed decisive but none of which in fact was; the Russian invasion, which, as with Hitler in World War II, was a decisive campaign; the global sea war and blockade which, if not decisive, was at least a major contributor to Napoleon's defeat through logistical attrition and mercantile loss; and the Peninsular campaign in which a small British army under the Duke of Wellington supported by Spanish and Portuguese regular and irregular forces bled the French for years, and ultimately invaded Metropolitan France itself by fighting its way across the Pyrenees. It was a campaign as important to Napoleon's defeat as the Allies' Normandy campaign was to the defeat of Hitler. The battles of Central Europe had their many French and German chroniclers; the Russian campaign was ever immortalized by Tolstoi's *War and Peace* and Tschaikovsky's *1812 Overture;* the sea war had an epic life to immortalize it: Nelson; only the Peninsular War remains unchronicled save for the fearsome paintings of Goya depicting the French atrocities in that brutal event.

Forester wrote of the European and Russian campaigns in *Napoleon and His Court* and *A Pawn among Kings.* Hornblower is Forester's correspondent to Nelson. *Death to the French* (1932; American title: *Rifleman Dodd)* and *The Gun* (1932) represent Forester's interest in and recognition of the importance of the Peninsular campaign, a war which did so much to bring down Napoleon.

In 1807 the Emperor Napoleon concluded a secret treaty with the Bourbon monarch of Spain allowing for the conquest of Portugal and its incorporation into Spain. A French army passed through Spain and seized Portugal, the royal family fleeing to Brazil. The Spanish king was coerced into surrendering his crown to Napoleon, who promptly bestowed it upon his own brother, Joseph. The Spanish revolted against the French just as the Portuguese were appealing to the British for aid in restoring their monarchy. Sir Arthur Wellesley, later Duke of Wellington, sailed for Corunna, Spain in 1808 with a British expeditionary force and an eight-year campaign resulted in the complete rout of the French and great glory to the British and their chief allies, the Spanish guerrillas.

Death to the French and *The Gun* both deal with small matters in a big, long war, but the war like many others was much affected by many seemingly minor incidents. In *Death to the French*, British Rifleman Matthew Dodd, in the year 1810, is cut off from his unit during a rear-guard action in Wellington's retreat to fortified lines around Lisbon. Dodd must find his way around the French army, through a denuded countryside, and back to his regiment, an apparently impossible task. He falls in with a party of Portuguese guerrillas and since he is a professional soldier and an expert rifleman, whereas they have little military experience and are armed with the inferior musket, he naturally becomes their leader. One might also be led to infer that Dodd's being English has something to do with his "natural" ability to lead and improvise when he is thrown alone into a situation requiring ingenuity, perseverance, courage, and command.

Unbeknownst to Dodd and his band, they have embarked on an individual war with a squad of French recruits led by a good natured, careful soldier, the not quite immortal Sergeant Godinot, who fails to shepherd his young charges through the brutal campaign despite his best and constant efforts. The British rifleman and the French sergeant are microcosms for Wellington and Napoleon, and Dodd's tiny campaign, in which all his Portuguese troops are killed, but which he survives, is a microcosm of the Peninsular War.

ﾠForester loves to depict the ironic in war. Dodd manages to burn a key French pontoon bridge before rejoining his regiment and for the rest of his life believes his action seriously affected and shortened the outcome of the campaign. The reader soon learns that the French high command had ordered the bridge destroyed and thus the bridge guard fought in vain to save the now unwanted and useless object.

The prose style of this book is perfectly suited for the simple story of simple men. Forester writes short, clear, journalistic sentences. His imagistic power is literal; it lies in direct description based on research, such as his account of a French supply train:

As far back as Dodd could see, and doubtless for miles beyond that, the road was jammed with wheel traffic. There were fifty guns and fifty caissons, there were the heavy waggons of the train, there were hundreds of country carts — the most primitive vehicle invented; each consisted of a long stout pole upon which was bolted a clumsy box-like framework of solid wood, much broader at the top than at the bottom. The wheels were solid, and immovable upon their axles, which rotated stiffly in sockets on the pole to the accompaniment of a most dolorous squeaking. Each cart was drawn by eight oxen, yoked two by two, goaded along by sulky Spanish or Portuguese renegades, and in each cart lay three or four sick or wounded Frenchmen, jolted about on the stony path, exposed to the rain, dying in dozens daily. Yet their lot, even so, was better than if they had been left behind to the mercy of Portuguese peasants.[1]

Carl Van Doren said: "What makes Forester exciting in the stories he tells is the candor with which he reports the incidents of the war."[2] The author omits no brutality, yet is never merely sensational. Every cruel or bloody incident is not only believable but important for the story. Dodd, like Brown and Allnutt, is short on words and deep thoughts, but long on ingenuity and character. Unlike Allnutt, he does not need a strong woman to stiffen him; his sense of duty and his loyalty to his regiment are enough. In other words, he is the perfect private soldier. When he finally makes his way back to his regiment, he is unable to explain to his superiors just what he has done and so he passes back into the ranks once more, another automaton on the firing line, his leadership ability and his intrepid ingenuity never again to be tested.

As a Napoleonic historian, Forester was at home in the Peninsular war and it was only natural for him to follow up *Death to the French* with a novel about the Spanish war effort in the north of the Iberian Peninsula. *The Gun* has as its "hero" a great bronze cannon, and except for the brief appearance of a Royal Navy captain, there is hardly an Englishman in sight. Forester shows how a particular piece of equipment, an object of war, can inspire courage, raise morale, foster ingenuity, and even seem to take on magical properties as it coalesces diverse elements and rival factions into a unified war effort.

The Gun's straightforward narrative style has the authentic air of a military dispatch. It is a professional piece of historical fiction with the ring of verisimilitude that marks the works of other great twentieth-century practitioners of the genre: Kenneth Roberts, Howard Fast, and James A. Michener. The *New York Times Book Review* called *The Gun* "vivid . . . a brilliantly imaginative reconstruction of the era of which it deals."[3]

A 6,000-pound bronze field cannon, firing eighteen-pound shot, has been abandoned by the regular Spanish army after its defeat at Espinosa. The gun is altogether too ponderous, but the peasant leader who eventually finds it decides to salvage it and employ it as a siege weapon against French fortifications. Eventually the peasants learn how to handle the piece and it becomes the nucleus for a 10,000-man irregular army led by successive guerrilla chiefs who fight among themselves as much as they fight the French. Finally the gun is superbly commanded and employed by an illiterate but clever peasant boy, but it is wrecked by French gunfire in an attack on an impregnable fort. The guerrilla army melts away but not until it has done irreparable harm to the French cause by disrupting the main line of French communication and relieving pressure on Wellington to the south in the fateful year of 1812. Forester is paying tribute to the Spanish will to preserve their independence from foreign domination. He realizes that despite Wellington's brilliant generalship and the strategic help of the Royal Navy, Napoleon would not have been defeated in Spain without the World War II–like partisan efforts of guerrilla forces.

Once again Forester has painstakingly researched military procedures as he would continue to do in all his historical novels. The reader relishes the details. The great cannon is not simply test fired. Instead:

One of the two reserve powder kegs was brought up and opened. A liberal measure of powder was scooped up and poured into the muzzle of the gun, a rammer which the armourer had prepared of a bundle of rags on the end of a pole was pushed up the barrel so that all the powder was packed into the breech, and then a piece of blanket was stuffed up after it to hold it firm. Next the armourer produced his masterpiece — a big round boulder selected from the bed of a stream and bound round with leather so as to fit the bore of the gun. This was pushed in on top of the wadding, and the gun was loaded.

At the armourer's order, half a dozen men laid hold of the trail, two others worked with levers at the wheels, and the gun was swung round until it pointed out of the quarry, across the road. The armourer mounted on the trail and fussed with the laying screw — which gave the necessary amount of fine adjustment in the lateral aiming of the gun which mere pulling round of the gun and carriage could not give with certainty. Looking through the notch on the bar of the back-sight he had made yesterday, the armourer aligned the groove on the muzzle swell with a patch of white rock showing through the undergrowth of the mountain side across the valley. Then he turned the elevating screw until the mark on the breech corresponded with the figure "250" on the elevation scale. The armourer had never in his life fired at such a range as two hundred and fifty *varas*, not even with the long Tyrolese rifle his lordship, the Marquis of Lazan, had brought him to repair before the war, but he estimated the distance as well as he could by the light of Nature. Next he scooped a little more powder from the keg, and with it filled the touchhole. Last of all he produced flint and steel tinder, caught, after many attempts, a spark upon this last, and transferred it to a length of slow match which he blew into a glow. All excitement, he was about to lay the match on the touchhole, when the harsh voice of El Bilbanito called him back. He was not to be the man to fire the first shot from the gun.[4]

Forester might have continued to chronicle the Peninsular War, a war with a hero but without an epic. Instead, he would choose the naval war against Napoleon for the background to his saga: but Hornblower could have been a British general, rising in rank and esteem in a long foreign campaign.

II The Peacemaker

In writing *The Peacemaker* (1934), Forester temporarily reverted to a contemporary English setting involving an uxorious, somewhat impalpable middle-class protagonist. Never again would Forester write fiction immediately concerning his own country in his own time. Beyond the local setting, the novel is much like an H. G. Wells fantasy. Edward Pethwick, a schoolteacher in an English private secondary school, with a doctorate in mathematics, is a brilliant but secretive physicist who had discovered the "Klein-Pethwick Effect," a combination of currents and coils possessing a contramagnetic effect. Pethwick has a henpecking, lower-class, alcoholic wife whom he does not love. His affections are for Dorothy, the young pacifist daughter of his headmaster. She falls in love with Pethwick, too, but his wife foils their Platonic love affair. In order to win Dorothy back and implement his own vague, pacifist concepts, Pethwick uses his discovery to paralyze London motor traffic while writing to the *Times* threatening further disruptions to society if disarmament is not immediately forthcoming. Instead of being considered a humanitarian savior of mankind, Pethwick finds himself branded as a criminal, especially after four children are killed in a panic resulting from the stalling of a train in the London underground. Pethwick's wife discovers his identity as the "Peacemaker" and he is stoned and trampled to death by an inflamed mob just as Dorothy returns from a Norwegian vacation, minutes too late to save her lover from his fate.

The novel is confusedly symbolic and allegorical. Forester seems to be damning both incompetent and impractical do-gooders as well as cynical controllers of power and makers of opinions. Also, there is the distinct antipacifist message that fanatic peacemongers may do more harm than good.

Once more in Forester's fiction a hero acts in part out of a sense of moral and class inferiority toward a woman: "Yet for all this, there was something Dorothy did not know about Pethwick. She did not know that he called her, to himself, 'a Lordly One.' She did not realise yet that along with the simplicity and modesty which she loved there existed a chronic sense of inferiority."[5]

The science-fiction aspect of the book, that a contramagnetic force in the form of an electrical wave could be developed and employed, is clever and well developed. The major weaknesses of the novel, however, are the stereotyping of all main characters and the weak passages of uncharacteristically purple prose reverting back to the excesses of the very first Forester novels:

The doors were all open in the hall. Dorothy could see the disordered sitting-room and kitchen, all the filth and evidence of neglect. There ran through her mind a memory of what her father had said — "a very brilliant young mathematician." And he stood there at the foot of the stairs, and the working of his face revealed the torment within him. He was clasping and unclasping his hands, and even in that light and at that moment Dorothy noticed their slender beauty. She was sick with unhappiness at the fate which had overtaken him, and it was revealed to her what horrors he had been through uncomplainingly. And she had always liked him, and now she more than liked him. She put out her hands towards his beautiful ones.[6]

For a moment Forester had taken a wrong literary turn. His next novel and all his subsequent long fiction would remain in the realm of historical and military writing, in which he was most at home.

III   The African Queen

In 1934 Forester's literary agent told him that a London newspaper had decided to publish novels in five-part serials with Monday to Friday episodes. Did Forester have a quick idea for serialization?[7] He hadn't offhand, but the money was good. Forester got on a train for his London suburban home. He started at the last car and walked forward. By the time he reached the first car the plot of *The African Queen* (1935) had formed in his mind, complete with the requisite five climaxes for serializations.[8]

The African Queen is a grand adventure story occurring in the autumn of 1914 in a place called "German Central Africa," which has a geography and history similar to the pre–World War I German East Africa, now the independent nation of Tanzania. There is a mythical, remote river called the Ulanga which passes through a series of practically unnavigable rapids and becomes the Bora River, which spreads out into an almost impassable delta, which itself drains into a lake called "Wittelsbach," after the Royal House of Bavaria. That body of water, apparently modeled after Lake Tanganyika, is dominated by an armed steamer of the Imperial German Navy, the *Koenigin Luise*.

Forester, of course, had never even gotten close to tropical Africa at the time of his life in which he was engaged in writing *The African*

Queen. However, it had become obvious to many reviewers and his readers that his skills as a writer had come to evidence a growing "gift for establishing verisimilitude."[9]

The heroine of *The African Queen* is Rose Sayer, the thirty-three-year-old spinster sister of an English missionary in German Central Africa. World War I has commenced. Her brother dies as the book opens and Rose is entirely alone on the mission station with her unburied brother, because the Germans, under the command of General Baron von Hanneken, have swept the area clean of all native people and livestock. The general appears to be an especially effective jungle commander, seemingly modeled after the great German colonial officer General Paul von Lettow Vorbeck of World War I fame.[10] Rose is without a survival plan when Charlie Allnutt arrives on the mission station. He is a familiar figure to her, a disreputable, unkempt, backwater colonial type found frequently in the pages of Joseph Conrad. The cockney Allnutt, who turns out to be remarkably good with all nuts and bolts, is the "captain" of the *African Queen*, a grandly named, but in reality worn-out thirty-foot shallow-draft steam launch, which has been deserted by her black crew.

Allnutt buries Samuel Sayer's body and suggests to Rose that they embark on the well-provisioned *African Queen* and take the boat to an island in the river to wait out the war's end or rescue by invading British forces. Charlie is not by nature a brave man. Rose disdains his natural cowardice and insists that they strike a blow for England by steaming downriver past the German fort, shoot the rapids, navigate the Bora, reach Lake Wittelsbach and sink the *Koenigin Luise* with blasting materials on the *African Queen*. Allnutt is appalled. Rose is totally ignorant of the impossibility of such a mission. Rose perseveres. Her patriotism is cynically viewed by Forester: "Rose stood at the tiller and steered out down the dark river mouth. They were off now, to strike their blow for the land of hope and glory of which Rose had sung as a child at concerts in Sunday school choirs. They were going to set wider those bounds and make the mighty country mightier yet."[11] In the beginning, Allnutt, like so many millions of his contemporary human beings, wishes only to survive the war, but he eventually is inspired to great heights of patriotic fervor by the mission and by his growing love for and devotion to Rose.

Their voyage is a terrible ordeal. Getting past the rifles of the German fort is child's play compared to their near shipwrecks, the

age, perseverance, indomitability, and unquestioning patriotism, she, nevertheless, is more human and thus more believable than even the greatest of Forester's fictional creations. Charlie Allnutt symbolizes, in Forester, the reverence intellectual man often has for manual man. If anything, Charlie is no thinker. Rose, who has had little opportunity to exercise her own mind, is easily able to manipulate him or bully him or cajole him into doing her bidding. However, he is an artisan and if he cannot think out the necessary projects to insure the success of their mission he can proceed on Rose's ideas. He is the invaluable engineer in modern society, gifted with tools. Rose's resolve, in motivating him to brilliant technological improvisations, simultaneously gives him courage, self-respect, and manhood. The despised weasel is forged into a man of commitment, worthy of loving and being loved.

The *African Queen* herself is almost a living character. Initially she is nearly comic: "The launch hardly seemed worthy of her grandiloquent name of 'African Queen.' She was squat, flat-bottomed, and thirty feet long. Her paint was peeling off her, and she reeked of decay. A tattered awning roofed in six feet of the stern; amidships stood the engine and boiler, with the stumpy funnel reaching up just higher than the awning."[18] The boat's boiler, which Forester inaccurately refers to as the engine, is something like an ancient and wounded espresso machine. Allnutt must tend it with great care: "He knelt in the bottom of the boat and addressed himself to the engine. He hauled out a panful of hot ashes and dumped them overside with a sizzle and a splutter. He filled the furnace with fresh wood from the pile beside him, and soon smoke appeared from the funnel and Rose could hear the roar of the draught. The engine began to sigh and splutter. . . ."[19]

However, the *African Queen* soon provides a microcosmic world which Rose and Charlie must save if they are to save themselves; it is the initial arena in which they must joust in the formation of their love relationship; it is the tiny sphere in which the intelligent woman, Rose, may exert a rightful leadership:

"Would you mind 'olding this tiller, miss, just as it is now?" asked Allnutt.

Rose silently took hold of the iron rod; it was so hot that it seemed to burn her hand. She held it resolutely, with almost a thrill at feeling the "African Queen" waver obediently in her course as she shifted the tiller ever so little.[20]

The *African Queen* is transmutted by the toil and suffering of her inhabitants into a plausible missile of war. She could have destroyed the *Koenigin Luise* if fate in the guise of the unexpected storm had not sunk her first and saved the German ship for a few days. However, it is as a ship of fools which becomes a crucible in which two lives are reshaped for the better that the *African Queen* achieves significance.

Now Forester has developed a finely honed, sparse style. There is no waste in this book in either plot or exposition. The atmosphere is convincing, the situation plausible if slightly strained. Forester keeps his art on sure ground, or should I say water? He is indeed in his element here. Forester and his first wife had journeyed extensively in a motor launch, as discussed in Chapter 1. Also, Forester could put to use his extensive knowledge of the events of World War I. Last, he ends *The African Queen* with a naval battle. The novelist is in complete command of his medium and thus he produces an exciting yarn and a viable, positive statement that men and women may indeed rescue love from indifference, and extract meaning from chaos even as the world turns so mad with hatred that nature herself seems to conspire with evil.

IV   The General

Lieutenant General Sir Herbert Curzon, K.C.M.G., C.B., D.S.O., like most generals, will die in bed, but he almost did not. In Curzon, Forester created a model of the archetypal military man, a figure that belongs to all ages and nations. Forester call *The General* (1936) his favorite book. He recognized his own best work, for *The General* is his masterpiece. As Erich Maria Remarque's *All Quiet on the Western Front* is the best fictional account of the horror and misery of the private soldier in World War I, so *The General* is the best fictional account of the mindlessness and brutal callousness of those who ran that war: the generals. Curzon is the prototype First World War officer, unbending, inflexible, and ignorant of the technology which in producing the machine gun and the tank, made the heroic cavalry charge with lance or saber and the infantry charge with bayonet equally obsolete. In their unwavering belief in the breakthrough, Allied and German generals condemned millions of young men to death on the Western Front, for "up until 1914 . . . through three major wars in which machine guns were employed . . . British military authorities remained stubbornly unaware of the inevitable consequence of the perfection of automatic weapons."[21]

The surviving generals did not even change after experiencing the 1914–1918 carnage, for as late as 1926 Field Marshal Douglas Haig, British Western Front commander from 1915 to the end of the war, could say, "I believe that the value of the horse and the opportunity for the horse in the future are likely to be as great as ever. . . . Aeroplanes and tanks are only accessories to the man and the horse. . . ."[22] It could have been Curzon speaking.

These then were the officers "who gave and took orders with the same undivided mind, and who passed up all cosmic conjecture in seeing to it that the line held firm. And hold firm it did, always, though every last man in it might be blown to bits. It was by such straight thinking tha the obscure cavalry major of 1914 became, within three years, one of the leading generals in the British army, with decorations on his uniform three rows deep."[23]

General Curzon is a son of middle-class parents who manage to send him to Sandhurst, the British West Point, and conveniently die, leaving him a small income. He is posted to the Twenty-Second Lancers, a good but not one of the best regiments of cavalry. The Twenty-First Lancers had made the last cavalry charge in British history at the 1898 battle of Omdurman in the Sudan war, with second lieutenant Winston Churchill leading a troop. Curzon wins a medal and promotion in the Boer War by good luck, muddling through, and his personal courage, which remains great during his entire life. When World War I breaks out, he is a forty-year-old major of cavalry. His regiment's colonel is too old to go into action in France, and so Curzon, to his great surprise, is given command of the regiment. He has all the qualities to lead men into battle except imagination. He is personally brave. He is scrupulously fair. He is above pettiness or jealousy. He obeys orders slavishly and demands that his orders are obeyed similarly. They are.

There was no limit to his savage energy in the execution of a clearcut task. He had no intention in the least of impressing his men with his ability to be everywhere at once, but that was the impression which the weary troopers formed of him. In his anxiety to see that every rifle was in action he hurried about the line rasping out his orders. The wounded and the fainthearted alike brought their rifles to their shoulders again under the stimulus of his presence. It was this kind of leadership for which all his native talents, all his experience and all his training were best suited. While Curzon was at hand not the most fleeting thought of retreat could cross a man's mind.[24]

Only a bullet or a shell can stop this sort of leader, who reacts to war with a series of conditioned reflex actions. Curzon is a taciturn, cold-blooded Englishman of the type that won the Empire and who did their duty as they saw it without question. "Here is . . . not a uncommon type of hero — the man who knows how to die magnificently, and does not in the least know how to live."[25] Thus the imbecility of war is to a large extent due to the traditions and training that created a fighting automaton with good military manners. Unfortunately, a Curzon can obey an order from a Hitler as easily as one from King George V.

Under Curzon's command the dismounted Twenty-Second Lancers conduct a heroic defense at the First Battle of Ypres at the cost of nearly the whole regiment. His superior is killed and Curzon succeeds to temporary command of the brigade, performing brilliantly in holding back the Germans. As an acting brigadier general, Curzon is sent back to train a newly raised infantry brigade despite the fact that he has spent his entire career in cavalry, but he has been singled out as a fighting general and there is great need for officers with combat success and singleminded determination. Before he can begin to work with his new command, he is selected to relieve a senile division commander and is promoted to major general. While on leave in London and full of confidence, he meets the spinster daughter of the influential Duke of Bude, Lady Emily; and after a whirlwind courtship, they marry despite the duchess's objections. The duke, however, approved the match, realizing that his daughter was past her prime and Curzon was a coming man.

In his next battle, Loos, Curzon's iron resolution leads to his being given command of an army corps and promotion to lieutenant-general. He sends thousands to their deaths at the battles of the Somme and Third Ypres without a qualm. The anticipated breakthroughs never materialize but Curzon is unshaken even when a relative calls him a murderer. Finally, his luck runs out and in the offensive of March 1918 the German army runs over and annihilates his corps. Curzon mounts his magnificent horse and rides out to meet death at the hands of the oncoming Germans. Instead, he is wounded by an exploding shell, loses a leg, and winds up spending the rest of his life in a wheelchair at Bournemouth, a fashionable seaside retirement resort. Sir Herbert and Lady Emily have lost their only son and were unable to have more children. Their life together was as sterile and fruitless as his military career.

Curzon cannot be loved, partly because he is incapable of loving.

His portrait is chilling. His personality is repelling. Yet the reader begrudgingly finds himself at least respecting this prototypical soldier, as one respects the integrity of fine steel. As a high-ranking general he has the rare opportunity for independent action and solitary command decision, Forester's favorite situation. Curzon, unable to bend with stress, proves brittle and breaks. He fails, his command is destroyed, he is maimed, and his life comes to naught. In that failure, Forester condemned a system and a generation of leaders. He said: "I wrote *The General* with the definite point of view that there had been considerable stupidity in the English army command during the last [First] World War. It was my aim to show what was bad, to point up what should be corrected. . . ."26

Forester's prose here is as tempered, spare, and keen as his cavalryman's saber. The fictitious battle of "Volkslaagte," perhaps based on the actual Boer War battle of Elandslaagte in 1899, illustrates Forester's combat reporter style:

Peering from the shelter of the rocks Curzon beheld the finest spectacle which could gladden the eyes of a cavalry officer. The gully had led him, all unaware, actually behind the flank of the Boer position. Half a mile in front of him, sited with Boer cunning on the reverse slope of a fold in the ground, was a battery of field guns sunk in shallow pits, the guns' crews clearly visible round them. There were groups of tethered ponies. There was a hint of rifle trenches far in front of the guns, and behind the guns were waggons and mounted staffs. There was all the vulnerable exposed confusion always to be found behind a firing line, and he and his squadron were within easy charging distance of it all, their presence unsuspected.

Curzon fought down the nightmare feeling of unreality which was stealing over him. He filed the squadron out of the gully and brought it up into line before any Boer had noticed them. Then, forgetting to draw his sword, he set his spurs into his horse and rode steadily, three lengths in front of his charging line, straight at the guns. The trumpeters pealed the charge as the pace quickened.

No undisciplined militia force could withstand the shock of an unexpected attack from the flank, however small the force which delivered it. The Boer defence which had all day held up the English attack collapsed like a pricked balloon. The whole space was black with men running for their ponies. Out on the open plain where the sweltering English infantry had barely been maintaining their firing lines the officers sensed what was happening. Some noticed the slackening of the Boer fire. Some saw the Boers rise out of their invisible trenches and run. One officer heard the cavalry trumpets, faint and sweet through the heated air. He yelled to his bugler to sound the charge. The skirmishing line rose up from flank to flank as bugler after bugler took up the call. Curzon had brought them the last necessary impetus for the attack. They poured over the Boer lines to where Curzon, his sword still in its sheath, was sitting dazed upon his horse amid the captured guns.[27]

Ultimately *The General* is a pacifistic work, a thesis novel that states with probity that war is a fool's game and, to paraphrase Samuel Johnson, patriotism is the last refuge of the hidebound. However, even as Forester was writing the last words of his second and last antiwar book, German militarism under the swastika was on the rise and war in Spain was beginning. Forester now abandons his antiwar stance and again turns to the Napoleonic period, this time to recast Britain's naval glory in a fictional mold, as if his artistic unconsciousness was beginning to sense his country's forthcoming need for hope and inspiration during the long night of war approaching. He has trained himself to excellence as an historical novelist and he is ready to use his art in the service of Western civilization.

CHAPTER 4

Hornblower: The Man Alone

C. S. Forester created Horatio Hornblower in 1937. Their association continued until Forester's death in 1966. It began as Forester watched a freighter captain, the skipper of the S. S. *Margaret Johnson*, make decisions for that little world he commanded, his ship.[1] It developed into a parable for English indomitability in the face of tyranny perpetrated by Napoleonic France or Hitlerian Germany. It ended as a fictional epic of a successful British naval officer, cast in the Nelsonian mold, who was born in obscurity on July 4, 1776, and who survived shot and shoal to live into an honored old age. In the process, Horatio Hornblower became one of those few characters in art who step out of the covers of a book or the arch of a proscenium stage seemingly to usurp an actual place in history. Sometimes those characters survive because they are true to life; Hornblower is true to history.

For Forester, the series were "psychological novels. They started with my interest in the problems of the independent command, they presented themselves to me in the first place as studies in psychology."[2] For his audience, the Hornblower saga represented the historical novel at its most exciting, an opportunity to identify with a Romantic hero and to learn a bit of history at the same time.

Perhaps the Hornblower Saga really began ten years before the first novel, *The Happy Return* (1937; American title; *Beat to Quarters*), was published. In 1927, in a secondhand book shop, Forester purchased three bound volumes of an old professional magazine, *The Naval Chronicle*, published from 1790 to 1820. The issues were written by naval officers for naval officers of the period and they served as a professional roundtable where ideas concerning tactics, shiphandling, communications, gunnery, and other naval procedures were discussed, shared, and evaluated. The books went with Forester aboard the *Annie Marble*, and as they represented his primary leisure reading for many months, the author absorbed them thoroughly and stowed away their copious information for a later day.

I *The Saga*

All in all, Forester wrote ten Hornblower novels, an eleventh which he was unable to finish before his death, and several additional stories which, some more than others, fit into the Saga. The most important of these stories is The Last Encounter," which Forester wrote as a conclusion to the tale of Hornblower. Almost all of the Saga were published first in serial form in the *Saturday Evening Post*, where they were lavishly and imaginatively illustrated. Some of the stories also appeared in *Collier's* and *Argosy*.

Mr. Midshipman Hornblower (1950) is, in fact, a collection of ten stories about the young Horatio Hornblower. It covers the period between June 1794 and March 1798. Horatio is seventeen when he reports aboard H.M.S. *Justinian*, becomes seasick immediately, and shortly afterwards is involved in a duel. Fortunately he is transferred to the frigate *Indefatigable*, under the command of the dashing Captain Sir Edward Pellew. Midshipman Hornblower is given the opportunity to bring a captured prize to port and promptly loses her. Captured by a French privateer, he sets fire to the enemy ship and effects her capture. His next learning experience is in a cutting-out expedition in which a French ship is stormed at her anchorage, captured, and sailed out. Then the young midshipman sees ship-to-ship action in command of the mizzen top. An unsuccessful attempt at a French Royalist invasion of Revolutionary France finds Horatio in action with British regular troops on the enemy shore. When the becalmed convoy, guarded by the *Indefatigable*, is attacked by Spanish galleys, Horatio captures one from a small craft. Promoted by Pellew to acting lieutenant, his examination for permanent promotion is interrupted and postponed by emergency action against Spanish fire ships at Gibraltar. He then has temporary command of a cattle boat. Finally, given his first real command, the tiny captured sloop *Le Reve*, Horatio is himself captured again, this time by the Spanish. His promotion comes through to him in captivity because of his outstanding service to date. The Spanish release him from captivity after he risks his life to effect the rescue of ship-wrecked Spanish sailors. In four years the young lieutenant has had an enormous amount of adventure and experience on which he would draw during his future career as a King's Officer.

One additional story is set during Horatio's midshipmancy. "The Hand of Destiny" takes place from October through December 1796. The story was published in *Collier's* on November 23, 1940, long before Forester thought of the possibility of a collection of Midshipman Hornblower stories. In it, Hornblower faces his first days as a lieutenant. He prevents a mutiny and thwarts a cruel captain. Clearly, Forester omitted "The Hand of Destiny" from *Midshipman Hornblower* because it conflicts chronologically and artistically with later work. For example, during "The Hand of Destiny," Hornblower is serving under a Captain Courtney on board His Majesty's Frigate *Marguerite* and they capture a Spanish vessel named the *Castilla*. In *Midshipman Hornblower* during the same period, Horatio is quite busy on the *Indefatigable*, under Captain Pellew. It is stated that he has been promoted to lieutenant at the age of twenty, whereas in *Midshipman Hornblower* he is promoted in August 1797 at the age of twenty-one, and while in Spanish captivity. Hornblower will fight another vessel named *Castilla* in *Hornblower and the Atropos* (1953). Last, in *Lord Hornblower* (1948) he would put down yet another mutiny, once more obtaining a free hand from his superior officer to deal with the mutineers. Forester simply cannibalized this story and used the material elsewhere. Then he ignored it nearly ten years later in planning and writing the stories which would comprise *Midshipman Hornblower*.

The events of "Hornblower's Temptation," first published in the *Saturday Evening Post* on December 9, 1950, and later included in *Hornblower during the Crisis* (1967), take place late in 1799 after his promotion, release, and restoration to duty. Hornblower is the junior lieutenant on H.M.S. *Renown*. He is given the onerous task of arranging for the execution of a man who is an Irish rebel and deserter by British standards but a hero to his own people. Hornblower agrees to forward the man's sea chest to his "wife" along with a letter and a poem. Eventually Hornblower discovers that the poem contains a coded combination for a secret compartment which holds a very large sum of money and a list of rebel names. Hornblower is tempted to turn over the trunk to his superiors but decides, in order to save the lives of the Irishmen on the list, to jettison the trunk and letter.

Lieutenant Hornblower (1952) introduces Hornblower's longtime friend and shipmate, Lieutenant William Bush. The story, covering

the period from May 1800 through March 1803, is told through
Bush's eyes. The *Renown* is commanded by the sadistic, schizo-
phrenic, paranoiac Captain Sawyer, who accuses his lieutenants, of
whom Hornblower is the most junior, of plotting a mutiny. Indeed,
they have been contemplating the possible need for a *Caine Mutiny*–type take-over. As Sawyer is about to arrest his officers, he
falls or is pushed down a hold. Suspicion seems to fall on Hornblower, who obviously is incapable of harming even a mad superior
officer, and also on a mistreated volunteer named Welland. Bush
and the reader never learn if Sawyer was pushed or actually fell,
although Welland's offstage drowning at the end of the book somewhat implies guilt and expiation.

With Captain Sawyer incapacitated by his fall, the first lieutenant,
Buckland, takes command. He is pusillanimous and finds it difficult
to make decisions. He finally reads the secret orders given to Sawyer
and orders an attack on the fortifications and privateer lair of Samana
Bay, Santo Domingo. Poorly planned, it fails, but Hornblower saves
the day with brilliant planning and courageous action. After cap-
turing the Spanish fortifications and all the defenders, the victorious
English embark all prisoners on the prizes and the *Renown*. The
latter is captured by escaping prisoners while enroute to Kingston.
Hornblower, skippering a prize, recaptures the ship of the line,
while Sawyer is killed by the Spaniards, Bush severely wounded,
and Buckland ignominiously caught and tied up in his bed.

In Kingston, Bush is hospitalized and Hornblower is promoted
to commander, subject to final approval at home. He is given command of a sloop and sent to England, where he arrives just after
news of peace with France, and so his promotion is not confirmed.

Bush returns to England, now paid off like most of the wartime
naval officers, to find Hornblower inpoverished, still a lieutenant,
without a billet, and eking out a mere subsistence in a club, playing
whist, an intellectual card game and the ancestor of bridge.

The reader and Bush meet Maria Mason, daughter of Hornblower's sharp-tongued landlady. Maria, who is dumpy and "not
quite young," is deeply in love with Horatio, who admires her and
appreciates her kindness but does not love her. Nevertheless, the
book's end finds Hornblower, to Bush's disgust, proposing to Maria,
having learned that war with France is about to break out again,
that his promotion is finally being confirmed, and that a command
is awaiting him thanks to a card partner who admires his brilliant
game, one Admiral Lord Parry, a commissioner of the navy.

The viewpoint in *Hornblower and the Hotspur* (1962) is the hero's once more. This work covers the period between April 1803 and July 1805. Hornblower is in command of the sloop *Hotspur*. His naval rank is commander. He has appointed Bush his first lieutenant. As the story opens, Hornblower marries Maria and proceeds to take the *Hotspur* on a long patrol to observe the French fleet at Brest as war approaches once more. Through brilliant seamanship he escapes from the guns of the French frigate *Loire* as war breaks out. Hornblower learns that Maria is pregnant. He plans and executes a successful attack on a French semaphore station and battery. Unfortunately, his steward proves to be a coward and the servant hangs himself in Hornblower's cabin. He is sent a well-trained servant, Doughty, who takes admirable care of Hornblower until the man makes a fatal mistake of striking a warrant officer in a quarrel. Hornblower reluctantly makes it possible for the steward to escape to the frigate *Constitution*, an American man-of-war in Cadiz, on her way to attack the Barbary pirates.

Meanwhile, Hornblower and the *Hotspur* survive a terrible winter on blockade duty and subsequently single-handedly thwart a French invasion of Ireland by smashing the transports. Then, given the opportunity to obtain vast prize money by being selected to participate in an action against a Spanish treasure fleet, Hornblower unselfishly chooses to take the *Hotspur* off to intercept the French frigate *Felicite*, attempting to warn the Spanish. Hornblower beats off the Frenchmen but loses all chance for the much-needed money, only to find later on that, although the treasure was captured, the sailors did not share the fortune due to a fine point of law. Maria has had a son, and when Hornblower returns to Plymouth she becomes pregnant again. As the book ends, Hornblower is recommended for promotion to captain and must leave the *Hotspur*.

Hornblower and the Crisis (1967; American title: *Hornblower during the Crisis*) deals with, or might have dealt with, the period between August and December 1805. Forester died before completing the work, althouth he left notes for the remainder of the book. The crisis is the impending invasion of Britain by Napoleon's amphibious forces which are waiting for Admiral Villenueve to achieve temporary control of the Channel. Meanwhile, the British nation is hoping that Nelson will be able to catch Villenueve at sea and destroy the French battle fleet.

As the story opens, Hornblower is just about to leave the *Hotspur*. He is relieved by Captain Meadows and he takes passage for England in a small supply vessel which, however, is delayed by adverse winds. While Hornblower is aboard the lighter, the *Hotspur* runs on a rock and is lost. Hornblower is a friendly witness at Meadow's court-martial. The latter received a reprimand and he winds up on the lighter with Hornblower with all the other officers from the *Hotspur*, including Bush.

The lighter, named *Princess*, is attacked by a French brig-of-war and, through Hornblower's clever plan and the courage of the English officers, the English get temporary control of the brig and escape. Meadows dies in the fight on the brig. Hornblower remembers to get the codes and dispatches from the cabin of the French captain.

Back at Plymouth, Hornblower brings the captured documents to the port admiral who sends him on to the Admiralty in London. Hornblower conceives a plan to copy and use the seals and Napoleon's signature from the documents to forge an order that, if delivered by British spies, would send Villenueve to sea, where Nelson could get at him. The Admiralty agrees to the plan, promotes Hornblower to captain, and sends him on the mission.

The plot continues in outline. Forester planned to send Hornblower to Spain with the forged order, where he would deliver it to Villenueve, who then would go to sea, only to be caught by Nelson at Trafalgar on October 21, 1805. Thus Hornblower would have been responsible for Nelson's opportunity to save England by ending the invasion crisis.

Hornblower and the Atropos (1953) encompasses the period from December 1805 to January 1808. Trafalgar has resulted in a decisive British victory and the death of Nelson. Maria is pregnant once more and the small family is traveling by canal boat from Gloucester to London. Hornblower is on his way to take command of the twenty-two-gun sloop *Atropos*. Although he is now a captain in rank, he is so junior that his new ship is still only a sloop-of-war, the smallest captain's billet in the Royal Navy.

To Hornblower's surprise, his first set of orders commands him to organize and execute plans for the funeral procession by water for the late Admiral Nelson. The main funeral barge, carrying the enormously heavy metal coffin, nearly sinks, placing both the hero of Trafalgar's body and Hornblower's career in grave jeopardy. Both "survive" the funeral by inches, for "never, *never*, would England forgive the man who allowed Nelson's coffin to sink, unceremoniously, in Thames mud beside the Isle of Dogs."[3]

At the very moment the funeral is taking place, Maria is giving birth to a daughter, their second child. Hornblower is presented to King George III. The king, sane at the time, orders Hornblower to take under his wing the royal great-nephew, the Prince of Seitz-Bunau, as a midshipman on the *Atropos*. With the Atropos at anchor in a fog, Hornblower rescues a British merchant ship seized by a French privateer, which he then captures. Hornblower sails for the Mediterranean, where he surmounts political, personnel, and technical difficulties to salvage British gold and silver from beneath the noses and guns of the Turks.

Another Spanish *Castilla* appears and *Atropos* joins with H.M. Frigate *Nightingale*, 28, to defeat and capture her. Hornblower takes *Atropos* to Sicily for repairs and there, unfortunately, the King of the Two Sicilies, having been driven from Naples by Napoleon and now shipless, desires a war ship and Admiral Collingwood finds it politically expedient to give the king the smallest ship in his command, the *Atropos*. Bitterly Hornblower returns to England to seek a frigate command, hopefully the *Lydia*, now fitting out. Arriving in Portsmouth, he rushes to Maria, only to find the children ill with smallpox.

Six months later Hornblower is at sea again on the *Lydia*, a thirty-six-gun frigate. *The Happy Return* (1937; American title: *Beat to Quarters*) covers some five months in Hornblower's career, June through October 1808. Bush is Hornblower's first lieutenant and we meet for the first time Coxswain Brown, and the woman who will be Hornblower's second wife, Lady Barbara. We also learn, late in the story, that Hornblower and Maria's two children have died of the smallpox attack related in *Hornblower and the Atropos*.

Hornblower has been ordered to sail the *Lydia*, 36, around Cape Horn to the Pacific Coast off Spanish Central America without making an intermediary port. The *Lydia* has been under sail for seven months and out of sight of land for eleven weeks. Hornblower achieves a miracle of navigation by making a perfect landfall anyway, arriving as ordered at the Gulf of Fonesca to meet with a mad Spanish rebel who calls himself El Supremo. Hornblower, with much distaste, supplies the rebel band with guns and ammunition and then captures the fifty-gun Spanish ship of the line *Natividad*, turning the valuable vessel over to El Supremo. Sailing South, Hornblower learns that Spain has taken herself out of the Napoleonic orbit and has allied herself with Britain. Now Hornblower must recapture the *Natividad*.

The situation is further complicated by the appearance of young

Lady Barbara Wellesley in Panama. She is the sister of the future
Duke of Wellington and thus one of the most influential women in
the British Empire. Lady Barbara, marooned in the Spanish pos-
session, insists on passage to England. Reluctantly Hornblower
accedes to her demands. However, despite her presence on board,
he must first find and defeat the Natividad once more. This time
she is better manned, and the rebels put up a courageous fight
before sinking. The damage to the Lydia is enormous and the Spanish will not help Hornblower repair his vessel, so Hornblower sails
her to a deserted island and completely refits the battered ship in
a mere sixteen days.

Meanwhile Lady Barbara has been a great help with the wounded,
and the taciturn captain falls in love with her. She loves Hornblower
and offers to become his mistress. The tormented hero cannot bring
himself to make love to her and the angered aristocrat sweeps out
of his life. The story ends with Hornblower on his way home to
Maria, seemingly relieved at having escaped commitment and scan-
dal.

A Ship of the Line (1938) covers the period between May and
October of 1810. Hornblower is in command of the ship of the line
Sutherland, 74, the "ugliest and least desirable two decker in the
Navy list." He has retained Bush as his first lieutenant. Meanwhile
Lady Barbara has married Rear Admiral Sir Percy Leighton and she
may have secretly used her influence to help obtain Hornblower his
new command, for the Sutherland has been assigned to Leighton's
squadron. Maria is pregnant once more.

The Sutherland is assigned to convoy duty and Hornblower saves
a fleet of East Indiamen from French privateers through brilliant
shiphandling. Temporarily on independent duty, he takes prizes,
destroys a shore battery, and even routs an army marching down
a Spanish road. Hornblower achieves five victories in three days.
When the flagship is dismasted and near to foundering in a fierce
storm, Hornblower tows the stricken vessel to safety in a fashion
similar to the way a ship of Nelson's was once saved by a subordinate.

Hornblower does not get on well with Leighton, who is not quite
up to his job. The admiral orders Hornblower to take command of
an ill-conceived and ill-fated Anglo-Spanish amphibious expedition
against the French fortification at Rosas. The attack fails and Hornblower barely escapes death. Finally Hornblower takes on four
French ships of the line in a desperate attempt to prevent them
from escaping Leighton's squadron. Although the French are

mauled, the *Sutherland* is shot to pieces, Bush's foot is blown off, and Hornblower surrenders the ship. As the book ends, Hornblower is facing years of captivity.

The story "Hornblower's Charitable Offering," which appeared in the May, 1941 issue of *Argosy*, may have been intended originally as a chapter in *Ship of the Line* and left out of the book by Forester perhaps because he finished it too late for inclusion, or it may have been an afterthought. The moment is sometime between May 16, 1810, when *Sutherland* departed Plymouth, and June 12, 1810, when she reached her squadron rendezvous off Point Palamos.

The *Sutherland* rescues two wretched French escapees from the Spanish prison island of Cabrera, where 20,000 French prisoners of war are being held without shelter and are near starvation. In an act of compassion, surely difficult to explain later on to the Admiralty, Hornblower lands a portion of his ship's food supplies to the pathetic prisoners.

Flying Colours (1938) picks up Hornblower's career immediately after the surrender of the *Sutherland* and covers the period from November 1810 through June 1811. Hornblower is a disconsolate prisoner at Rosas. The four damaged French ships and the stricken *Sutherland* are at anchor beneath his fortress prison. He witnesses their destruction by British fire-ships.

Hornblower is to be sent to Paris with Bush to stand trial for "piracy" by order of Napoleon. It is expected that Hornblower will be executed. Hornblower selects Coxswain Brown to accompany them as his servant during the long and arduous winter coach trip under guard through the heart of France. Bush is feverish because of the amputation of his lower leg and Hornblower and Brown struggle to keep him alive on the cruel trip. The coach runs off the road in a snow storm and, seeing a rowboat at the riverside, Hornblower seizes upon an escape plan. The Englishmen overpower their chief captor and steal the boat. They drift down the unknown river until capsized at a waterfall.

Miraculously they all survive and make their way to the first house in sight, where to their good fortune they are sheltered by an old royalist, the Comte de Graçay, and his young, widowed daughter-in-law, Marie. Four months later, the lady becomes Hornblower's lover. In the spring, the Englishmen attempt to escape from France by building a fifteen-foot, flat-bottomed boat (the same length as the *Annie Marble*), and rowing down the Loire to Nantes, where, disguised as Dutch officers loyal to the French, they recapture the

British cutter *Witch of Endor*, 10, and, with the help of released prisoners of the French, fight off pursuers and sail the vessel to the British channel fleet, where Hornblower is welcomed as one thought to be dead. Bush is immediately promoted to commander.

Hornblower soon learns first that Leighton is dead and then that Maria died giving birth to a son who has survived. In England the routine court-martial acquits him with honor. Hornblower is taken to London and is invested as a Knight of the Order of the Bath by the Prince Regent. He is also awarded a sinecure pension as Colonel of Marines. Now affluent and famous, but still not happy, Sir Horatio calls on Lady Barbara, who has been caring for his infant son, Richard. *Flying Colours* ends with Hornblower knowing "she was his for the asking," and the clear implication that he would ask.

Commodore Hornblower (1945) opens with Horatio and Barbara married and living in the manor house of Smallbridge. The book covers the period between May and October 1812. Hornblower is promoted to commodore and ordered to take a squadron of vessels to the Baltic to harass the French forces, protect British maritime trade, show the flag, and exert diplomatic pressure on the Swedes and Russians in the British cause. Hornblower is now a player on the great stage of European diplomacy. He is given the seventy-four-gun ship of the line *Nonsuch* for his flag and, at his request, one-legged Bush is made captain of the flagship, serving as Hornblower's second in command.

Towing a disabled bomb ketch, Hornblower's squadron forces its way into the Baltic past enemy batteries. He recaptures a prize and cleverly destroys the French privateer *Blanchefleur* with mortar fire from his two bomb vessels. The action, in Swedish waters, so angers Napoleon that he seizes a piece of Sweden, alienating that nation.

Hornblower sails to the Russian naval base at Kronstadt, where he stiffens Czar Alexander's resolve to resist Napoleon. Hornblower thwarts his Finnish-born interpreter's attempt to assassinate the czar and Prince Bernadotte of Sweden. Getting slightly drunk at an imperial banquet, Hornblower makes love to the Countess Canerine. She gives him fleas.

Operating in the Baltic, Hornblower harasses Bonaparte's northern flank. Ordered to Riga to prevent one of Napoleon's armies, under the command of General Macdonald, from reaching the northern Russian capital, St. Petersburg, Hornblower meets the countess once more but remains sober. At the siege of Riga, Hornblower serves with Colonel von Clausewitz, the great military theorist, who has defected from the Prussian army under Napoleon's control and is aiding the Russian stand against the tyrant.

Hornblower's bomb ketches blast Macdonald's siege and field artillery, gaining more time for the Russians. Hornblower then plans and executes a successful amphibious operation. Caught up in an enemy attack, Hornblower, on horseback, saves the Russian defenders by leading them in a flanking counterattack. The Russian army and the British naval squadron hold Macdonald at Riga while Napoleon meets his destiny at Moscow, but Hornblower is physically exhausted by his exertions. Finally, as Macdonald retreats, Hornblower has a feverish inspiration and he gallops with Clausewitz after the Prussian army in Macdonald's force. Hornblower convinces the Prussians to defect from Napoleon, thus changing the entire course of the war. Hornblower has practically saved Russia and caused Prussia to switch from the French to the British cause. However, he has contracted typhus and the squadron sails home without him. Recovering, he makes his way home to England and Barbara's arms.

The events of the story "Hornblower and His Majesty," published in the March 23, 1940, issue of *Collier's* and the March 1941 issue of *Argosy*, take place sometime during the period from late 1812, when Hornblower ostensibly has recovered from his illness and is back on duty, and December 24, 1815, the date of peace between Britain and the United States, and the end of the War of 1812. Here Forester is careless about dates or arithmetic, and Hornblower's Baltic command, not having been written as yet, is of course ignored. Since Forester mentions recent single-ship-action victories by the United States, the time most likely is the end of the first six months of the War of 1812, sometime in January 1813. Sir Horatio is given command of the royal yacht *Augusta* and ordered to take the mad but lovable King George III for a healthful sail up the English Channel.

The royal yacht is surprised and chased by a Yankee privateer. Hornblower is tempted to surrender with the thought that the capture of the king might bring about an end to the unnecessary war between Britain and America. Putting temptation aside, Hornblower effects an escape into a fog bank.

Lord Hornblower (1946) extends over the period from October 1813 through May 1814. Hornblower is called upon to suppress yet another mutiny. This time the men of the brig *Flame* have imprisoned their cruel captain and threatened to sail the ship into French hands if they are not given amnesty and redress. Commodore Horn-blower is assigned the sister ship of the *Flame*, the brig *Porta Coeli*, and he obtains orders to negotiate. He locates the mutineers off Le Harve and is unable to convince them to give up. Hornblower tricks the French into driving the *Flame* towards him, and in a brilliant hand to hand boarding Hornblower leads the recapture of the *Flame* and the acquisition of a French prize.

A French prisoner suggests that the mayor of Le Harve might be able to cause the war-weary city to defect in exchange for commercial privileges. Hornblower sends for reinforcements and to Horn-blower's delight, Captain Bush arrives with the *Nonsuch*, 74. The city is secured and Hornblower becomes governor (an early Douglas MacArthur) of a French port with a Bourbon duke as figurehead ruler. Hornblower waits for a French counterattack. He sends Bush up the Seine to attack and destroy the French siege train, and although Bush is successful, he is killed when the powder barges blow up. Hornblower is disconsolate at the loss of his best friend through his orders.

Immediately, Barbara arrives with additional French royalty. Napoleon is finally defeated and Paris is taken. Hornblower is re-warded for his seizure of Le Harve by elevation to the peerage. He is now Lord Hornblower of Smallbridge. In Paris, Barbara is asked by her brother, the Duke of Wellington, to go to Vienna with him and serve as his hostess as he represents England at the Council of Vienna. Barbara is delighted, but Hornblower refuses to accompany her, partly out of jealousy for his brother-in-law's achievement and partly because there would be nothing for him to do there. They quarrel.

Before leaving for Smallbridge, Hornblower meets his old friend the Count de Graçay, and his former lover, Marie, for whom his feelings rekindle. The timing is dangerous for his marriage and career.

With Barbara in Vienna, Hornblower returns to Smallbridge but is soon restless. He and Brown decide to visit Graçay at the count's invitation. He and Marie become lovers again while Brown marries a young French girl. Suddenly their reverie is interrupted by the news that Napoleon has escaped from Elba and the Bourbon army has deserted to Bonaparte. France is Napoleon's again and Horn-blower, the count, Marie, and Brown must flee for their lives. Asked to lead a guerrilla uprising, they forfeit their chance for escape but manage to tie down a division of French troops sorely needed by Napoleon in the North. In the moment of their capture, Marie is shot to death., The count and Hornblower are sentenced to be shot, and as Hornblower awaits execution at dawn he is told, "It is not death." Napoleon has been defeated at Waterloo. This time the war is truly over and he will return to Barbara and his son, Richard.

"The Point and the Edge" is merely an outline of a story which Forester relates in *The Hornblower Companion* (1964) as an example of his writing technique.[4] Hornblower, in the year 1819, is a very senior captain keeping busy and fit on the beach by taking fencing lessons. He is nearly mugged by a destitute thug but he defeats and captures the mugger with the point of his walking stick. Instead of having the man arrested and executed, he has him enlisted in the Royal Navy. Forester either never actually wrote out the story or it was never published and subsequently lost or destroyed.

Hornblower in the West Indies (1958; American title: *Admiral Hornblower in the West Indies*) covers the period between May 1821 and October 1823. Hornblower is now a rear admiral and has been given his first full flag assignment as commander-in-chief of the British West Indies Squadron. It is peacetime and the squadron consists of only a few frigates, brigs, and schooners. Yet there is much to do. In New Orleans, Hornblower learns of a French plot to rescue Napoleon from St. Helena and return him to the throne of France, with the probable further outcome that the world would be torn by war once more.

Hornblower thwarts the plot by lying to General Count Cambonne, commander of the Old Guard. He tells the general that Napoleon is dead, giving his word of honor as a gentleman that he speaks the truth. The French are diverted from St., Helena and the despairing Hornblower returns to base to resign his commission because of his loss of honor, only to find that Napoleon has indeed died. Hornblower's long, personal conflict with Napoleon is finally over and the world is saved from the scourge of war.

In the next episode, Hornblower captures a speedy Spanish slaver by cleverly having a drogue attached to the faster ship's rudder. Then Hornblower is kidnapped by pirates in Jamaica, and after his release he destroys their lair using mortar fire once more.

Hornblower then is a witness to the victory of General Simón Bolívar at the turning point of the war for Venezuelan liberation, the Battle of Carabobo on June 24, 1821. His sympathies are with the rebels, who are aided by British mercenaries.

After his three-year tour of duty is at an end, Lady Barbara comes out from England to meet him in Kingston and return home with her husband. Hornblower is saddened by the end of his command. He has, of course, performed brilliantly. Upon being relieved of command, Hornblower and Lady Barbara take passage on a packet ship bound for home. The *Pretty Jane* runs into a fierce hurricane and nearly founders. Only a waterlogged cargo keeps her afloat. Hornblower takes charge and through his courage, seamanship, and intelligence he saves Barbara's life and the lives of the surviving crew. In the face of imminent death, Barbara confesses that she never loved her first husband and that she has only loved Hornblower. After their safe arrival in Puerto Rico, Hornblower realizes that Barbara's words have made him happy forever.

In the early 1960s Forester wrote the story "The Last Encounter" as a conclusion to the Hornblower Saga, and then he deposited the manuscript in his bank vault, probably desiring its publication after his death. It was published with *Hornblower and the Crisis* (1967). The story is set in 1848, the year of revolution. Hornblower is now seventy-two, healthy and wealthy, recently promoted to Admiral-of-the-Fleet, although he can never expect active duty again. Lady Barbara is well and still beautiful. Brown continues to serve as Hornblower's butler, although a long time ago he substituted "Ye, my lord," for "aye, aye sir." Son Richard is a colonel in the guards serving the young Queen Victoria, and there are promising grand-children.

On a rainy night a man comes to Smallbridge announcing that he is "Napoleon Bonaparte" and asking the loan of a horse and carriage to get him to the next train station so that he can rush to Paris to meet his destiny in the forthcoming elections. Old Hornblower is sure that the man is mad, but is amused that someone should impersonate, albeit badly, his old, long-deceased adversary. The stranger flatters Lady Barbara and she talks Hornblower into indulging the request. Later it turns out that the visitor was indeed a Bonaparte, Prince Louis Napoleon Bonaparte, nephew of Napoleon I, Pretender to the Imperial Throne, soon to be President of France and eventually Emperor Napoleon III. Once more Hornblower has influenced history. Thus with a humorous tale, the Saga of Horatio Hornblower comes to a happy conclusion.

In 1964 Forester published *The Hornblower Companion* containing charts of the Hornblower adventures drawn by Samuel H. Bryant with Forester's comments on the locales and "Some Personal

Notes." The latter is an account of Forester's writing techniques and a history of how he came to create and develop Hornblower.[5]

II   *Writing the Hornblower Saga*

Forester did not set out in 1936 to write a novel epic. Hornblower came into being as the answer to a set of problems devised by a working novelist as he pursued his craft in the subgenre of the historical novel. Hornblower became almost a living character, and Forester spun out the Hornblower Saga in part because of the circumstances of the novelist's life, because of the initial growing demand for the reading public for more Hornblower, and because Forester found in Hornblower an alter-ego, a surrogate life of action to complement his own life of the mind, his own life of ever-decreasing physical activity.

Not surprisingly, the origin of the Hornblower Saga lies in both chance and Forester's penchant for eclectic and esoteric research. The second-hand purchase in 1927 of the three volumes of *TheNaval Chronicle* from 1790 to 1820, to be read and reread aboard the *Annie Marble,* provided Forester, along with continuing interest in the Napoleonic war and the Peninsular Campaign, with the seeds for the Saga. Forester also studied Sir Charles Oman's magnum opus, *A History of the Peninsular War* (1902–1930), after writing *Death to the French* and *The Gun*. Finally, although he never mentioned it in his brief autobiographical writings, Forester must have become acquainted with the life and career of Admiral Lord Donald Cochrane and perhaps read either Cochrane's autobiography[6] or the biography written by his heir, Thomas Barnes Cochrane.[7] Cochrane was probably the greatest frigate captain in the history of the Royal Navy and surely one of its most outstanding seamen. The parallels between Cochrane's real life and Hornblower's fictional life are almost startling. Their dates are similar, Cochrane having been born in 1775 and having died in 1860. Cochrane performed convoy duty in frigates and on several occasions saved English merchant ships from French coastal privateers as Hornblower does in *Ship of the Line*.[8] Cochrane used signal and flag ruses as Hornblower does in *Ship of the Line* and the tactic is used unsuccessfully against Hornblower in *Commodore Hornblower*. Cochrane once took on three French ships of the line with only one small ship at his command and damaged them considerably before surrendering, as Hornblower does in *Ship of the Line*. Cochrane, in sloops or frigates, defeated much more powerful ships, as Hornblower does in *The Happy Return*. Cochrane fought dockyard corruption, as Hornblower attempts to do in a small way in *Hornblower and the Atropos*. Cochrane conducted extremely successful amphibious actions against enemy signal stations, shore batteries, and harbors with prizes to cut out, as Hornblower does while commanding both *Hotspur* and *Sutherland*. Both Cochrane and Hornblower are harassed by bureaucrats for supposedly excess use of powder and shot expended in the King's service. Cochrane was a friend of the Wellesley family. Like Hornblower, Cochrane destroyed a French army column ashore by brilliant inshore shiphandling and outstanding gunnery. Cochrane planned and led a great fire-ship action similar to the one Hornblower observed at the beginning of *Flying Colours*. Cochrane was made Knight of the Bath by George III in 1809, Hornblower in 1811. Both Cochrane and Hornblower obtain command of the West Indies Station. Cochrane planned a rescue of Napoleon from St. Helena in order to make him Emperor of South America. Hornblower thwarts a rescue attempt in *Hornblower in the West Indies*.

However, although both Cochrane and Hornblower were superb navigators and as commanders were adored by their men, their backgrounds and personalities differed. Cochrane was a nobleman by birth and, although beloved by subordinates, was hated by superiors because of his arrogant, uncompromising, and overweening manner. Hornblower was never disrespectful to superior officers no matter what he thought of their abilities. Hornblower's career, when compared to Cochrane's, actually seems more plausible. Yet both the wild lord and the careful, middle-class mariner end their lives as Admirals-of-the-Fleet, the highest rank in the Royal Navy.

Only Lord Nelson, also a middle-class mariner, can claim to have more influence over the writing of the Hornblower Saga than Lord Cochrane. Forester wrote a biography of Nelson before he created Hornblower. In some ways the Hornblower Saga is almost a biography of Cochrane.

The details provided in *The Naval Chronicles* intrigued Forester. In them he not only learned of naval campaigns, ships' encounters, and diplomatic accomplishments, but also of shiphandling, maneuvers, stationkeeping, signaling, gunnery, heavy-weather sailing, courts-martial, punishment, and execution. He learned in full detail the texts of treaties such as the Treaty of Ghent, which ended the War of 1812. In a sense, by reading and rereading the *Chronicles* and other related books, Forester trained vicariously as a British naval officer of the Napoleonic period.

Observing the captain of the *Margaret Johnson* at work, the Man Alone, in command, making decisions sometimes of a life-and-death nature, but much more often of routine and business, Forester conceived the idea of an historical novel set in the Central American waters he was then visiting in a leisurely manner. It would be a naval story, probably because Forester was at sea, for he was also fascinated by the character of the Duke of Wellington, who certainly could have illustrated and provided a situation of exploring the problems, challenges, and possibilities of the Man Alone as he led the isolated British Expeditionary Force in the Iberian Peninsula. But a sea story it would be, one partially set in the Gulf of Fonesca, where the *Margaret Johnson* anchored and Forester did some power boating. If Wellington would not figure in the novel which would be *The Happy Return*, an imaginary younger sister, Miss Barbara Wellesley, would. The Wellesley family had had its scandals. Nelson, of course, had been involved with Lady Hamilton. Perhaps the fictitious sister might have a fictitious naval lover?

The world of 1936 was obsessed with the break-up of Spain and the rising tide of war. In comparison, Forester thought of the break-up of the Spanish Empire in Bonaparte's time and immediately afterwards, a break-up in which Nelson and Cochrane had participated. Queer things had happened on the Central American coast. Could the British, in their desperate attempt to wrench Spain out of the French orbit in 1808, have supported a demonic rebel, one who might call himself El Supremo? Thus the first character of the Hornblower Saga was born, and he was not Hornblower, the hero, but El Supremo, the villain.[9]

Finally, as the *Margaret Johnson* entered the Atlantic, the British naval captain, who would be a victim of the Spanish change of sides following Napoleon's attempt to put his brother in the throne of Spain, and who would have to first befriend and then battle El Supremo, began to develop. Hornblower was to be Forester's main example of the Man Alone. The writer would send his protagonist on independent duty far from home and diplomatic support; and further complicate matters for the tested officer by placing an influential noblewoman aboard the captain's man-of-war. That ship would have to be a frigate, for ships of the line seldom operated independently, anymore than battleships did in World War I or World War II.

Without intending to create an epic hero of eleven volumes' duration, Forester, nevertheless, from the beginning set a particular task for himself. Although his hero would conquer his country's enemy or enemies in time, his internal struggles, his cynicism concerning his own motives, his human weaknesses, and his occasional despair would engage him in internal combat for a lifetime. Never would that struggle entirely subside into self-satisfaction.[10]

Hornblower was not to be an aristocrat, thus making the affair with Lady Barbara more complicated and more interesting. He would be in his early thirties, married to an uninteresting and less than attractive woman, whom he seldom managed to see due to the demands of his profession. Most of all, however, the hero, soon to be named Horatio Hornblower, would be a perceptive, imaginative man, brave but not fearless, a superb leader, through which the reading public would be able to see the events and actions of the novel. He would also be shy and unsure of himself socially, a somewhat tall and gangling man, handsome in an unselfconscious, rugged, masculine way. He would get tongue-tied and seasick. He would be a whiz at mathematics and be totally tone-deaf. *The Happy Return* was then written with comparative ease and Horatio Hornblower was born seemingly to live out his fictional life in one year and one book.

After the acceptance of *The Happy Return*, Forester continued to study the Peninsular War and the way British seapower had strangled Napoleon's attempt to reinforce and supply by sea his fortresses in Spain. Simultaneously, Forester was growing more and more interested in General Francisco Franco's revolt in Spain. The author decided to write a sequel to *The Happy Return* in which he could portray the effectiveness of the British blockade in 1809–1810. Hornblower was to be resurrected and given command of a ship of the line and sent to the Spanish Coast, where he could again use his knowledge of Spanish, first ascertained in *The Happy Return*. He would help Wellington in thwarting the French design for Spain. But this time Hornblower was not to be so successful. It was one of Forester's most important decisions, in writing *Ship of the Line*, to insure that Hornblower would not always be victorious, at least not at first. He would lose Lady Barbara to Admiral Leighton. He would be one of the few English captains ever to surrender a ship to the French, and the novel would end with his career in shambles, with Hornblower parted, seemingly until the long war ended, from both his wife and the woman who had nearly been his lover.

With Hornblower a prisoner of the French in a Spanish fortress, Forester began to read some of the letters of Napoleon. The letters revealed to Forester that Napoleon was essentially unscrupulous in nearly all his dealings, a nineteenth-century Machiavellian and practitioner of *Realpolitik*. Napoleon could be "induced" by the novelist to condemn the imprisoned British captain as a pirate because he had employed a ruse of war in sailing under false colors. The ruse was legitimate but Napoleon could still make political capital out of it. Perhaps there could be an escape arranged for Hornblower, but how could this occur if Hornblower and the wounded Bush were to be transported to Paris for a travesty trial and with almost all of Continental Europe in Napoleon's hands? The problem was fascinating for Forester and *Flying Colours* resulted.

The difficulty of finding a way for three Englishmen to escape from the middle of France, with one of them recently relieved of a foot, was resolved by Forester's recollection of his boating trip years before on the River Loire in the *Annie Marble*. Forester's experiences afloat were never as a yachting sailor but rather as a river and canal boatsman. He would put the three escaping Englishmen, Hornblower, Bush, and Brown, into a small boat and float them down a river. The title of the book was, in fact, suggested by the publisher, Michael Joseph, who said to Forester, "You want to bring him back with flying colours?"[11] Once Forester got his escapees down to the port city of Nantes, he knew Hornblower could find a ship and sail them all safely home again; but what fun to have his hero no longer in command of a mighty ship of the line, but temporarily skipper of a twenty-foot boat and a crew of three.

Forester decided at this time to kill off both Maria and Admiral Leighton so that there would be no impediments to the marriage of Horatio and Barbara. Yet despite his love affair with Marie de Graçay and the unexpected intimacy with Bush, Hornblower remained the Man Alone, keeping his own counsel always, in command and solely responsible.

It was six years between the writing of *Flying Colours* and *Commodore Hornblower*, years in which Forester struggled with crippling arteriosclerosis and depression. The thought of continuing his hero's active life, just as his own active life had been curtailed, appealed to Forester. However it was bomb ketches that really caught his attention. Forester had developed a fascination for those strange, ill-used, two-masted, mortar-carrying vessels of the Napoleonic period. They had been used frequently in amphibious operations, the kind of affair Hornblower rather excelled in. Their special value was that they could lob an exploding shell shoreward in a high trajectory, rather than merely send a solid shot a short distance on a flat trajectory. The bomb ketches presented the first realistic shore bombardment possibilities. Forester had witnessed the effective use of modern long-range gunnery in shore bombardment aboard an American battleship in 1943, just prior to his illness. He decided to plan a hypothetical ship-to-shore campaign with bomb ketches and larger vessels to cover the mortars. Of course, Hornblower was ready to command the squadron. He was ready for promotion, too, to commodore. And he had been trained by Forester as a Man Alone, now ready to make strategic as well as tactical decisions, ready to deal with friendly nations as well as neutrals and enemies. The place was the Baltic, the year was 1812, the book was *Commodore Hornblower*. Of course it was better for Forester, with his millions of American readers, to have Hornblower in the Baltic in 1812 rather than off Baltimore that fateful year.

Commodore Hornblower first came out in serial form in the *Saturday Evening Post*. Forester was never quite sure that his work was well suited for that kind of publication and later on the Hornblower books would suffer somewhat because of their episodal construction forced on them by the length limitations and the need for chapter or section climaxes. As a general and family magazine, the *Post* required a degree of sanitizing and decorum not expected in general fiction in the 1940s through the 1960s. Nevertheless, Hornblower's adultery in *Commodore Hornblower*, albeit a one-night stand under the influence of drink (Commodore Hornblower could never hold liquor well) and punished by the infestation of fleas, was the first adultery in the history of the *Post* and it provoked numerous newspaper comments and letters from the reading public. Did Forester mean to imply that the typhus Hornblower contracted, a disease passed on through lice, might have been transmitted in the act of adulterous sexual intercourse and was perhaps a punishment on the Adventurer by the God-Novelist for his first infidelity to Lady Barbara?

Hornblower's recovery after typhus paralleled Forester's partial recovery from arteriosclerosis, or at least the disease had halted and the author had learned to live with his disability. He also had been disabled.

It was now 1945 and Forester was witnessing the break-up of the three Axis empires. With Hornblower safely back at Smallbridge,

Forester began to reflect on the fall of the Napoleonic empire. It must be remembered that the first five of Forester's Hornblower books were written either just before or during World War II. In the writing of *Commodore Hornblower* and *Lord Hornblower*, Forester used Napoleon as a surrogate Hitler. Both men had been archenemies of England, both had conquered almost all of Continental Europe, both had been kept at bay by the British Navy, and both had come within inches, or rather the few miles of the English Channel, of conquering Forester's beloved country. Now Forester turned with relish to Hornblower's part in the defeat, if not in the death, of the villain who had longed for his blood.

During the last days of Napoleon's reign, the city of Bordeaux had defected from the emperor's cause. Forester thought it might be an interesting task for his Man Alone to be involved in the defection of a French city, to have to run it, supply it, defend it, as many an Allied commander had done or was still doing in Europe, Asia, and Africa. After all, some, like General Douglas MacArthur, had whole nations to administer.

Now Forester decided to complicate the relationship between Horatio and Barbara. By having them go their separate ways from Paris after Hornblower meets Marie once more, Forester is able to start up the romance between Hornblower and Marie again and to create a situation in which Hornblower is trapped in France during Napoleon's brief return to power before the Battle of Waterloo. *Lord Hornblower* turned out to be the most carefully crafted and precisely motivated of the Hornblower novels, the one which satisfied Forester the most. It builds to great suspense and ends only a minute or so after Hornblower has been reprieved from certain death.

Soon after completing *Lord Hornblower* and believing he was finished with the naval hero, Forester suffered a severe and near fatal heart attack. He was only given an even chance to live. Once more Forester turned to the Hornblower Saga for therapy. He decided to write on the young Hornblower's beginning, with his entry into the Royal Navy as a midshipman. Remembering his even chance to live or die, Forester created a depressed young man willing to take an even chance in a duel, either to rid himself of a tormentor or be killed and thus end an unbearable existence. It was also pleasant to imagine Lord Hornblower as a young man, eighteen years old, navigating French prizes, skirmishing with Spanish galleys, eventually taken prisoner, and conveniently learning Spanish in preparation for previously written adventures aboard the *Lydia*. Hornblower seemed to confer some of his youth on his creator, who rallied and recovered. Thus, *Midshipman Hornblower* was written as a labor of therapy and love.

It was only natural for Forester to begin to fill in further gaps in the Saga between Midshipman Hornblower's career and Captain Hornblower's adventures. *Lieutenant Hornblower* followed the midshipman's story. Forester had found a copy of a British militia artillery manual of 1860 and he became very interested in the use of heated shot by coast artillery against wooden ships. He wanted to put that information into a novel. Forester could also pay homage to Hornblower's doughty friend Bush, sadly dispatched in *Lord Hornblower*, by letting the good lieutenant, his shot-away foot temporarily restored, tell this story. Now Forester could also explain Hornblower's rather improbable marriage to Maria. Hornblower is then promoted, loses the promotion because of peace, is in despair, and then regains the promotion with the renewal of war with France. He is a commander, but the readers will not see Hornblower acting in that rank until much later.

Now Forester skips from 1803 to 1805 and he will have to back and fill later on. But in *Hornblower and the Atropos* he can link up with *The Happy Return*. Hornblower is to be a very junior captain, too junior to have commanded a ship of the line, alas, at Trafalgar, but of just the right seniority to be given charge of the water section of the funeral arrangements for Nelson. Forester can also use his knowledge of the inland waterways of England. He had spent much time on the English canals and rivers in a motorboat. Now he could combine this knowledge with his interest in exploring further the relationship between Hornblower and Maria, whom he had killed off in *Flying Colours*. And then the two children had to die. The little happiness they had brought Horatio was over and Forester could feel quite satisfied that although Hornblower had been given much happiness with Barbara and his third child, Richard, he had earned his family bliss with his early unhappiness and suffering.

After *Hornblower and the Atropos*, Forester had the opportunity to sail in the West Indies. In those lovely, warm waters he got to thinking about Hornblower again. His hero was not one to remain happy for long, and it was time to consider his career after the end of the Napoleonic wars. Perhaps, given the long, peacetime wait between commands, Hornblower at Smallbridge would begin to brood over Barbara's first marriage. Did she love Leighton, or his memory, more than she loved him? Better to promote him to rear admiral and to send him to sea again. The West Indies kept the shrunken Royal Navy busy enough in the 1820s. There was a great deal of fighting going on in Central and South America, the slave trade was under attack from the Royal Navy, piracy needed suppression, and finally there was the odd fact located that some of Napoleon's Old Guard had seized a piece of Texas from Mexico and had tried unsuccessfully to colonize it. Perhaps they could be inveigled into an attempt to free their old master on St. Helena and return him to the throne of France? Of course his nemesis, Horatio Hornblower, would just happen to be Commander-in-Chief of the West Indies Squadron and the one to thwart such a sinister design. Most important of all for the Hornblower Saga is the fact that Forester used *Hornblower in the West Indies* to finally cement the bond between Hornblower and Barbara. Forester brings the development of that relationship to fruition and culmination in the great storm scene. Their love is on firm ground forever. The next and last appearance of Lady Barbara is as a contented old woman in "The Last Encounter."

Forester had finished with Hornblower's active service with *Hornblower in the West Indies* and he had to back and fill once more. Fortunately, there was a significant gap in Hornblower's early career to be filled in. Hornblower had not been seen in the rank of commander and the period from 1803 to 1805 should have found him in a sea command distinguishing himself enough to obtain the rank of captain and command of the *Atropos*. *Hornblower and the Hotspur* resulted. The incident of the forfeited prize money actually occurred in 1804, and the *Hotspur's* seakeeping blockade off France was based on the actions of small ships of the Royal Navy during that very period. Hornblower was at his best in single-ship, Man Alone situations. Commanding the *Hotspur* brought out the finest in Hornblower and, indeed, the best in Forester., Although episodal, *Hornblower and the Hotspur* is perhaps the most tightly knit and believeable of the Saga.

But if time could be played back and rerun for Hornblower it could not be for Forester. The novelist decided to write "The Last Encounter" as a wrap-up story and put it away until after his death. Then, almost as an afterthought, Forester went to work on a long Hornblower novel once more. At last Forester would deal with the one precise time in the naval history of the Napoleonic Wars he had assiduously avoided: Trafalgar. Hornblower, who already had been

made to attend Nelson's coffin in *Hornblower and the Atropos,*
surely would have had at least something to do with England's
greatest naval victory. A few months in 1805 remained available for
some action by Hornblower and Forester decided to have his hero
bring about the decisive action at Trafalgar by espionage work, since
he apparently could not have been at the battle, due to the lack of
enough chronological time to develop a command situation between
Hotspur and *Atropos.* So Forester died with Hornblower in action
in *Hornblower and the Crisis* and on his way to force the French
to fight Nelson. Thus he is still in transit, with Maria and their first
son and Bush alive; and with the joys of Lady Barbara yet unknown.

III   *Scope and Accomplishment*

The Hornblower Saga masterfully evokes a time, the Napoleonic
Wars; a milieu, the life of a British naval officer of the epoch; and
a place, the British world of the Romantic period. Forester takes
his readers on a world tour during what was, in fact, a world war.
We freeze in the Arctic and swelter in the Caribbean; we smell the
stenches of rotting corpses, gunpowder, filthy bodies, excrement
in the holds, and opulent food at imperial courts. Bullets and cannon
shot miss us by inches; the sea is ever waiting to swallow us. Death
comes suddenly and violently to our friends at our sides. But, like
Hornblower, we survive shot and sharpened sword point, the worst
the angry ocean can do, the perfidy of our enemies and even despair
over the death of those we love. Always there is Forester's ultimate
skill: he makes us believe we are there.

The effect was achieved because Forester mastered the quintes-
sential skill of the historical novelist; the mixing of fact and fiction,
of real personages and fictional characters, of actual events and
plausible events which seem as if they could have happened at a
circumscribed time and in a real place. Furthermore, and of great
importance, there was Forester's intuitive realization that the historical novelist's success is directly proportional to his ability as a
background painter. The historical panorama must appear unseamed
and flawless to sustain the "suspension of disbelief."

The Hornblower novels are, for the most part, heavily plotted on
carefully constructed outlines. The reader's attention is quickly captured, and even when the novel is episodally constructed for serialization the storyline and the character interest carry through.
Young readers today, picking up a paperback Hornblower, very

frequently find themselves searching out additional titles until they have read the entire Saga, for above all the Hornblower books bring great pleasure to every class of readers.

Forester created a superb, ever-developing protagonist. When Hornblower first appears in *Flying Colours* he is something of a supersailor. His navigation is miraculous and he is able to defeat the ship of the line *Natividad* not once but twice. Something of a caricature, he is short-tempered and given to making odd sounds rather than communicating with people. Hornblower was created and first flourished in the period just before and during World War II, a time when many people in the world were looking for great heroes, perhaps almost comic book superheroes, as the war against the unmitigated evil of totalitarianism took shape. It was a time when men and women would most admire the military leader for his martial virtues. Generals and admirals were the most applauded of men: Montgomery, Eisenhower, MacArthur, Zhukov, Halsey, Nimitz, Patton, and even Rommel.

As time passed and the end of the war brought a waning of enthusiasm for the military man, Hornblower changed, became more human, more fallible. Midshipman Hornblower and Lieutenant Hornblower could make and did make errors; Commander Hornblower in *Hornblower and the Hotspur* is at his most complex, and in his most interesting person. Hornblower is a man living in a more disillusioned world.

With *Hornblower in the West Indies*, Forester was able to capture the British sense of having become a declining world sea power, so that the admiral has only a few small ships for his squadron and, like an old and almost toothless lion, uses cunning instead of strength. Wits would have to serve for power, even at the risk of honor. Thus, intuitively, perhaps, Forester made his hero serve the popular needs of his time and his audience by molding Hornblower into a reflection of the British, and even perhaps the American self-image.

Finally, Hornblower was a hero cut out for the mass audience. He illustrated the Romantic notion of advancement through merit. It was perhaps Forester's most manipulative alteration of probability to have a poor physician's son rise not only to high rank in the caste-ridden Royal Navy of the Napoleonic period, but even to marry into the first rank of nobility, something which even Nelson had not done. It was very gratifying for the millions who read the Saga to believe, however, that a humbly born man of integrity and ability, modest, and highly self-critical, loyal almost to a fault, could overcome such dangers and adversities as Hornblower did, could survive shot and prison fever, captivity, and a dictator's enmity to rise to the top of his profession and achieve his nation's esteem and the love of a brilliant, beautiful, influential, and rich woman.

If *Hornblower and the Hotspur*, with its brooding and suffering hero doing the grimmest duty of war, is Forester's best Hornblower novel, then *Hornblower in the West Indies*, except for the emotional recommitments of Horatio and Barbara at the end, is Forester's weakest, due not only to its jarringly episodal nature, but also to its strained improbabilities, especially the unmotivated and unprepared escape of Hornblower's secretary from Cockpit Country in Jamaica. But no Hornblower novel is a great art novel. It is as a total effort, the historical novelist recreating an epoch on a grand scale, that the importance of Forester's work here can best be understood and appreciated. Like Shakespeare with his historical octology of the Wars of the Roses from their first cause in *Richard II* to their conclusion in *Richard III*, Forester came to his subject without an overall plan. It was an idea which grew on him, and he, like the great playwright, would back and fill to finish placing an historical vision on paper. This is not to compare Forester with Shakespeare, of course, but only to point out that an epic may develop almost as if it had a mind of its own, or perhaps because there was created an indomitable character who won a stranglehold over his creator and would not die. This character, Horatio Hornblower, was both a masterful tactician and a superb strategist; an outstanding naval leader; and diplomat who could see the grand plans of early nineteenth-century Europe even as he led men into battle on sea and land; a benevolent commander; a legendary officer who though firm with his subordinates was nevertheless loved; a nervous man; a self-doubting man; a poor lover, perhaps; a worse husband, sometimes unfaithful; in sum, a hero of great scale, who, however could be identified with by millions of ordinary mortals living long after Horatio Hornblower's time.

Thus the adventures of Horatio Hornblower from *Midshipman Hornblower* to "The Last Encounter" form a body of literature that will most probably outlast not only Forester's best work, like *The General*, but most of the art novels of the author's time. Succeeding generations shall not weary of a well-written story. They will come to know that within the covers of a Hornblower book a wind is forever rising, a dark sea beginning to boil, and a few brave men commanded by an intrepid if dour leader are setting out under oars in a wooden longboat toward a hostile shore in service to a good cause. The sand appears beneath the keel, the trees above the beach take shape, there is the glittering reflection of steel in the woods, and then—but who knows—but that in the end, beyond the daring adventure, all will be well. That certainty, along with the rich consistency of character and Forester's narrative skills, may prove that there is a place in popular reading for novels which do not rely on crass sentimentality, soft-core pornography, or unmitigated violence in order to give pleasure, to offer insight into human behavior, and to evoke simultaneously the immediateness and the distance of the past.

CHAPTER 5

The War Storm: 1937–1946

ALTHOUGH the stormy years of the Spanish Civil War and World War II found Forester deeply involved first in journalism and then in Allied propaganda, they were nevertheless prolific ones for the novelist. During these painful years, when most creative artists found it difficult to produce their art, with so many living in exile and often despairing of a victory over one of history's greatest evils, Forester published eight novels and a children's book: *Poo-Poo and the Dragons* (1942). For Forester, these years were particularly creative and experimental. In them, he and Hornblower found each other; and this coming together resulted in five Hornblower books, some half of the Saga. Forester's three other novels of the period were each experimental in that they each broke new ground for him. *The Earthly Paradise* (1940; American title: *To the Indies*) is Forester's first attempt at biographical fiction; that is, writing a novel based on the life and times of an historical person. *The Captain from Connecticut* (1941) applies the techniques and information used in the Hornblower Saga to an American subject. *The Ship* (1943) is Forester's first effort to assimilate and use his shipboard experiences of World War II in long fiction.

I Fictional Biography

In *The Earthly Paradise* Forester tells the story of Christopher Columbus's third voyage to America, which began on May 30, 1498, and which was personally his most disastrous, the voyage from which he returned in chains. The book title is ironic, of course. Columbus set out to find the earthly paradise, literally the Garden of Eden. The peaceful Amerindian world he discovered and ruined was a warless paradise beneath his eyes, but which he never saw for his visions of biblical sites and the wealthy realm of the fabulous Khan.

Europe had begun Word War II as Forester wrote this book. It seems the earthly paradise of the New World so quickly ruined by the Spaniards was an allegorical equivalent of the world of 1939 being brought to destruction by the greed and hatred of contemporary man.

Forester tells this tale of Columbus through the eyes of a strange character, Don Narciso Rich, an attorney representing the interests of King Ferdinand and Queen Isabella. He is fat, celibate, base born, not overly brave, and forty; quite out of place with the young, frustrated grandees embarked with Columbus and him on board the *Holy Name*. Because of past experiences, Columbus is loathe to trust anyone, but eventually the honest Narciso wins his confidence. Though a landlubber, he studies navigation; though naturally a follower, he learns to lead; though inexperienced in war or hardship, he perseveres and becomes the unlikely hero of the story, all the time, however, commenting on the actions of Columbus. It is Narciso who discovers the mouth of the Orinoco River and the mainland of South America. It is Narciso, the sole survivor of a hurricane and ship wreck, who finds himself the solitary inhabitant of a *Robinson Crusoe*–like island, and who manages through skill, courage, and cunning to return to Hispaniola (Haiti) and safety. Yet it is Narciso who must write the secret report to the king and queen pointing out that although Columbus is a great navigator, he is a dismal failure as a leader and dangerous as an administrator. So, ironically, it is the one man who Columbus trusts who causes the old visionary's downfall and disgrace. On the very ship in which the regenerated lawyer returns to Spain, the pitiful explorer is brought back in chains.

In his growth as a person, Narciso learns to doubt authority: the authority of the great navigator who refuses to believe that a continent is a continent because it does not "fit" his scheme of the world; the authority of a Church that tortures and burns Indians in the name of a merciful God; and the authority and supposed infallibility of the ancient didactic scientists like Pliny, the naturalist. Narciso grows hard and lean of mind and body in his adventure of discovery of himself. He changes from a medieval to a modern man.

Columbus, on the other hand, who leads his new expedition to Trinidad, then to the Gulf of Paria, and then to the mainland of South America, all for the first time, is a dreamer whose recurring and increasing dreams of locating the great Khan, the Fountain of Youth, the Garden of Eden, the Golden City of Cambaluc, and the

Tree of Knowledge, increasingly debilitate him until he can no longer exercise proper authority and he is gulled by almost everyone from his brother to his ex-valet. Columbus is sad and pathetic. Forester does not choose to make him a hero; he is a flawed John Brown, a fanatical visionary, who would have been a superb sailing master for a fleet of exploration, but a man doomed through leadership flaws to fail as a viceroy of a new empire. As a Man Alone, Columbus is the ultimate failure in Forester's work. He has little of Nelson or Hornblower; even his basic goodness falls victim to his need to prove success with gold extracted by the slave labor of Indians.

A religious reader is forced to contemplate that God indeed chose to work in a wondrously strange way when He selected Christopher Columbus to discover the New World for Europe.

Once more, Forester is at his best in describing battle scenes, as in the Spanish-Indian battle on the plains of Hispaniola:

"Fire!" yelled the *Adelantado*.

The crash of the handguns drowned the noise of the discharge of the crossbows. Rich saw one Indian fall, and next moment the two nations were at grips. The Indians carried heavy sticks for the most part, with which they struck clumsily at the helmets in front of them, clumsily, like clowns in a comedy. Perched up on his horse Rich caught vivid glimpses of brown faces, some of them striped with red paint, distorted with passion. He saw the expression on one turn to mild dismay as a Spaniard drove his sword home. Rich's horse was chafing at the bit as the smell of blood reached his nostrils; close in front of him a crossbowman was winding frantically at his moulinet. There came a loud bang as one of the recharged handguns went off, and then another and another. The brown masses began to hesitate, and ceased to crowd up against the sword-points.

"They're going to break!" said the *Adelantado*. "Gentlemen, are you ready?"

The crossbowman thrust his loaded weapon forward between the two swordsmen who were protecting him, and released the bolt with a whizz and a clatter.

"Open up when you charge, gentlemen. Ride them down and show no mercy," said the *Adelantado*. "There! They're breaking! Sailors, make way! Open your ranks sailors! Come on, gentlemen!"

The sailors, who formed one face of the square, huddled off to either side making a gap for the horsemen, who poured through it in a torrent, the maddened horses jostling each other. Rich kept his seat with difficulty as his horse dashed out along with his fellows; reins and sword seemed to have become mixed in his grip. Avila was riding in front of him, his horse stretched to a gallop and his lance, with its fluttering banderol, in rest before him. The point caught a flying Indian in the back below the ribs, and lifted him forward in a great leap before he dropped and spread-eagled on the ground; and Avila rode forward to free his point. The swords were wheeling in great arcs of fire under the sun. There was an Indian running madly close by Rich's right knee, his hands crossed over his head to ward off the impending blow. Rich had his sword hand free now, and he swung and struck at the hands, and the Indian fell with a dull shriek.[1]

Despite Forester's continued ability to evoke a time or place with consummate credibility, *The Earthly Paradise* is not a totally successful work. The problem exists in the shifting focus of the novel. Ostensibly, Forester set out to offer a biographical treatment of the great explorer in a fictionalized setting. In the process of writing the book, Forester shifted his focus from the often weak-willed and always dogmatic discoverer to the ever-changing, ever-hardening conquistador who can come to enjoy bloody repression, after first showing great humanitarian concern for the treatment of the Indian. "Rich was a little ashamed of his pity for the Indians; this bold talk of suppressing rebellion was much more the sort of thing he felt he ought to like. All his life so far he had lived as a spectator, and there was something peculiarly gratifying in being at last behind the scenes, in being at least a potential actor. It was better than splitting legal hairs and wrapping up the result in pages of Latin."[2]

As the character of Columbus lacks depth, dimension, and verisimilitude, whereas Don Narciso Rich does not, so the book is less than fully successful in its apparent motive: to offer insight into the development, activities, and achievements of Christopher Columbus. One critic, Ben Ray Redman of the *Saturday Review of Literature*, argued that "Don Narciso is unequal to the central role."[3] He was not intended for center stage, Columbus was. Thus the book structurally sags, like a ship with a weakened keel. Forester would not attempt to fictionalize history again this way until he would write the more successful *Hunting the Bismarck* (1959).

II   *The American Hornblower*

The Captain from Connecticut (1941), coming as it did quite soon after Forester's success with the Captain Hornblower trilogy, was an abortive attempt to create an American Hornblower in the person of Captain Josiah Peabody, United States Navy, veteran of the Quasi-War with France and the War against the Barbary Pirates, and now, in the winter of 1814, in command of the frigate *Delaware* (seemingly based on the career of the frigate *Constellation* in the War of 1812). The ship is about to run the British blockade of New York so as to be the last American warship in the Atlantic. The mission is almost a suicide one and the book begins with high drama and the possibility of fascinating characterization in the person of Peabody and his younger brother, Jonathan, a midshipman but tempermentally ill-suited to the sea. Unfortunately, the story deteriorates into improbabilities and an unbelievable cliff-hanger ending.

Peabody is an excellent naval commander, a fine example of the Man Alone, able to make successful, individual judgments, and carry out his orders with imagination, courage, skill, and daring. He is worthy of Hornblower, even if he is as not colorful. Like Hornblower, too, he has had little experience with young women and he is susceptible to beautiful, aristocratic ladies. Peabody's New England Puritanism, brought to fruition in him by his impoverished Connecticut farm upbringing, his tyrannical father, and his early victory over alcoholism as a young officer, (a disease his own mother suffered), is akin to Hornblower's stoicism in motivating, effecting, and manifesting character and action. Peabody is almost as taciturn as Hornblower. He is as self-critical; unfortunately, however he is the only fully developed character in the novel.

In a blinding snow storm, the *Delaware*, thanks to Peabody's superb seamanship, slips by the British blockading squadron off Sandy Hook, under the command of Nelson's old friend Captain Hardy. At sea, Peabody heads the *Delaware* toward the Caribbean, where, in conjunction with two small American privateers, he mauls the British West Indies convoy by engaging and crippling all three British warships guarding the convoy, one vessel at a time. The commanding officer of the British squadron is Captain Sir Hubert Davenant, R.N. of H.M.S. *Calypso*, 36, a near match alone for the *Delaware*. Davenant, a beefy, choloric naval stereotype, becomes Peabody's antagonist for the remainder of the story. The early naval encounters of the book are "described with a literary craftsmanship that makes one oblivious of the author's remarkable technical knowledge of ships and naval operations of the day."[4]

Escaping the battered enemy squadron, the *Delaware* becomes a very effective commerce raider until the British find her again and she is trapped off Martinique. Peabody squares off to fight the three dogging ships to the death when the impending hostilities are interrupted and superceded by French authorities, Martinique being

French once more after the recent fall of Napoleon and the restoration of the Bourbon dynasty. The French governor, backed by the guns of his fortress, refuses to allow the ships to fight in French territorial waters and they must anchor in the harbor of Fort-de-France to fulfill neutrality requirements.

The antagonists are trapped in Martinique. There, at a dress ball, Peabody meets and falls in love with his noble host's lovely daughter, Anne de Villeboix. She loves Peabody, too, and, with the *Delaware* facing mortal combat as soon as she clears Fort-de-France, the couple marry despite the feeble objections of Anne's father. Meanwhile, to Peabody's mortification, his brother deserts the American Navy to marry a wealthy Frenchwoman. The major flaw of the book is that the Jonathan Peabody subplot remains unresolved. Peabody is unable to take action to bring about the return of his brother to the ship for trial and the book ends with Jonathan unrepentent, unpardoned, and unpunished. Forester simply neglects to deal with him.

Up to the point that the British squadron and the *Delaware* are trapped in Martinique, the book races along at a delightful pace with the reader luxuriating in battle scenes, sailing descriptions, and shipboard routine. The story then loses credibility even for Romantic fiction. For example, a duel between Peabody and Davenant ends without a casualty because Anne has substituted toast for the bullets, unbeknownst to the participants. It is a device Forester would use again in *Midshipman Hornblower*. Also, declaring a lengthy truce, the British and Americans go off together to fight a notorious pirate, allowing Forester to write another battle scene towards the end of the novel with his hero struggling manfully in hand to hand combat and receiving sword cuts from the pirate captain, whom he subdues. At the end, the British and the Americans set out again to fight to the finish, only to learn at the last moment that peace has been made and they can be friends. Last of all, the reader learns that Davenant will marry Anne's aunt. The book's final words find the British captain saying, "We'll celebrate the peace together." Peabody replies: "Yes, Uncle."[5]

Forster has particular trouble with the depiction of women in this novel. All females are two-dimensional. Anne is especially disappointing and without definition or substance. As one reviewer pointed out: "whenever the rustle of silk supplants the thunder of sail and attention centers on the Governor-General's sister or the Governor's daughter, 'as lovely as the set of the *Delaware's* foretopsail,' the author's characterization reflects something of the self-consciousness the sea officers show in the company of the ladies. His rapture seems more convincing when he dwells on the fore-topsail and not the lady."[6]

Despite the fact that most of *The Captain from Connecticut* is set in the West Indies, Forester treats blacks as background objects, lumping them together as the "negroes" in the scene. The two exceptions do him little credit. Peabody's obsequious manservant, Washington, unlike Hornblower's English steward, is comic and stupid. The fine description of personal combat between the black pirate captain, Lerouge, and Peabody is marred only by racial stereotyping:

The blades rasped harshly together, jarring his fingers as they gripped his sword hilt, and only in the nick of time did he beat aside the first thrust which Lerouge had made. This was death, death in the hot sun; the loud noises of battle which he heard about him reached his consciousness as faintly as the squeaking of mice.

Lerouge's mirthless grin, as his thick lips parted snarling, appeared to grow wider and wider until Peabody seemed to see nothing else. The sword blades slipped apart, and Peabody made a wild blind effort to cover himself. There was a sudden burning pain in his right forearm, and his sword hilt escaped from his paralyzed fingers. Desperately he leaped forward; chance—or his own rapid instinctive reactions—put Lerouge's sword blade into his left hand, low down by the guard, and he tore the weapon out of his path as he closed with his powerful antagonist. . . . He put out all his strength for the fall, was balked, swayed to his left, and heaved again in one last insane effort. Lerouge's feet left the deck, and he fell with a crash, Peabody staggering above him with the sword in his left hand and the golden threads of the torn-off epaulette in his right.[7]

In general "the characters are supplement for romantic narrative, but they are without depth and have only elementary psychology. . . ."[8]

Forester may have indeed contemplated a series parallel to the Hornblower books with an American captain as his hero. If so, he abandoned the idea, possibly because *The Captain from Connecticut* ends with the cessation of hostilities in the War of 1812. Of course, Forester could have backed and filled with stories of Lieutenant Peabody in action off Tripoli or serving under Captain Thomas Truxtun in the Quasi-War with France. Most likely, however, Forester was less than fully satisfied with *The Captain from Connecticut* and with the remaining possibilities in the characterization of Peabody.

The author was not as much at home with the New England sensibility as he was with that of his own countrymen. Hornblower presented a more artistically fruitful course to follow. Forester may have thought that a Peabody saga would make him more ·money with the larger American reading audience. In the end, however, he totally won the American market with Hornblower.

However, Forester would return to the War of 1812 as a subject periphally in Hornblower stories but also centrally in *The Age of Fighting Sail* (1956). Looking at the naval war from the American viewpoint, and considering that he wrote *The Captain from Connecticut* at a time that Britain was already in World War II and the United States close to allying herself with that country, Forester concluded that the war was unnecessary. It never would have occurred if President Thomas Jefferson had permitted substantial naval development in response to Tripoli's declaration of war in 1801. A powerful American squadron of ships of the line, built to suppress Barbary piracy, would have deterred British aggression against American commerce at a time when Great Britain was fighting against Napoleon for her survival.

III   *World War II in Fiction*

Doing his part for the British war effort by working for the British Ministry for Information gave Forester opportunities to embark in allied warships and it was expected that besides writing journalistic pieces he would put his talents as a fiction writer to use in the service of his country. The first result was *The Ship* (1943), one of the better sea novels of World War II.

It is always difficult for a writer to serve a patriotic cause and simultaneously be true to his art. This is so because most propaganda requires sharp contrast between the values and also the people of both sides, with one set being portrayed as exemplar and the other as unmitigated evil, whereas the artist intuitively realizes that life, and therefore true art, is not so pat. *The Ship* probably succeeds more than most other war novels written during World War II in simultaneously serving a cause in a blatant fashion and remaining an authentic piece of fiction which the author would not have to disavow after the frenzies and the passions of the war had cooled.

More so than even in *The African Queen*, Forester makes a vessel, H.M.S.*Artemis*, the heroine of his tale. The *Artemis*, loved by her 600 sailors as men may have loved her chaste and beautiful namesake, is a British light cruiser on convoy duty in the Mediterranean Sea in 1942. The story of one day in the life of the *Artemis* is told in twenty-six short chapters with each chapter built about phrases from the terse and modest Captain's Report after the battle. Diana Trilling called the book "a perfect encyclopedia of naval information, only accidentally fictionalized, but fascinating technical reading."[9] For Forester sets out to make modern naval warfare, in all its complexities, comprehensible to his wartime audience.

As the story opens, the *Artemis*, as part of a squadron of British light cruisers, is guarding a vital convoy on its way to Malta, the besieged island fortress which is hanging on by a thread and thwarting Field Marshal Erwin Rommel's campaign to conquer North Africa and the Middle East in order to link with the Japanese and end the war in Axis victory. The British are desperate but, as ever, cool. During the morning the *Artemis* and the other escorts had fought off an Italian air attack. Now they must do battle against impossible odds, because an Italian fleet of battleships and heavy cruisers has been sent to intercept and destroy the convoy. At all costs the light cruisers with their six-inch guns must keep the battleships with their fourteen-inch weapons away from the convoy.

The British lay down a smokescreen and dart in and out of it, attacking the Italians and retreating again and again, hoping that night will fall before the escorts are destroyed and the convoy bombarded. With courage, experience, determination, superior shiphandling and gunnery, the British, by scoring many more shell hits than the enemy can, manage to force the stronger Italian force to turn away and break off battle, thus saving the vital convoy. The *Artemis* is hit twice, many men are killed, but she remains in action, her decks aflame, but fighting to the bitter end of the engagement.

Much of the action is seen through the eyes of various officers and ratings and much of the book is devoted to disgressions into their lives and backgrounds, for *The Ship* is as much a book about the British character as Forester saw it in World War II as it is about a ship in action.

First of all, there is the captain: Captain the Honourable Miles Ernest Troughton-Harrington-Yorke, R.N., son of the seventh Earl of Severne. (Troughton was Forester's mother's maiden name.) Although an aristocrat by birth, he has worked his way up from midshipman to his captaincy through merit. He is a dedicated, competent, intelligent, intrepid naval officer, beloved by his men. He has trained his crew to a fine point and his acute sense of duty allows him to face possible death and the destruction of his command with equanimity

Then there is the captain's secretary, Paymaster Sub-Lieutenant James Jerningham, a former junior advertising executive who misses his many girl friends and who believes himself lacking in courage. He isn't. Only his sensitivity and intelligence cause him to think about pain and death while others act instinctively. The reader is continually brought away from the ongoing battle by digressions into the thoughts of the various men who are fighting, the pom-pom gunner, the ship's electrician, the lookout, and many others. We learn of their hopes and dreams. Some of them die before our eyes. Forester is showing his audience that every casualty listed in a bulletin or news report represents a human life as important and meaningful as the reader's. Ultimately war is fought by men and women with fragile flesh and blood and minds, and not by their servant machines.

In *The Ship* Forester's descriptive powers are at his height. The book is filled with evocative, even breathtaking passages, as when the *Artemis* is described:

> In H.M.S. *Artemis* a high proportion of the brains of the ship was massed together on the bridge: Captain and Torpedo Officer, Navigating Lieutenant and Officer of the Watch, Asdic cabinet and signalmen. They stood there unprotected even from the weather, nothing over their heads, and, less than shoulder-high round them, only the thin plating which served merely to keep out the seas when the ship was taking green water in over her bows. Death could strike unhindered anywhere on that bridge; but then death could strike anywhere in the whole ship, for the plating of which she was constructed was hardly thicker than paper. Even a machine-gun bullet could penetrate if it struck square. The brains might as well be posed on the bridge as anywhere else—even the imposing-looking turrets which housed the six-inch guns served no better purpose than to keep out the rain. The ship was an eggshell armed with sledge-hammers, and her mission in life was to give without receiving.[10]

Forester is particularly competent in providing interesting descriptions of mechanical or technical matters, so vital to the fighting ship, in a way so as to make these descriptions central to the developing sense of ship's character, function, and purpose. *Artemis* shoots this way:

> the pointer moved on the dial, and the turret rotated its heavy weight

smoothly as Gunlayer Wayne kept his pointer following it. As the pointer coincided, with the guns loaded, the circuit was closed which illuminated the "Gun ready" lamp before the eyes of the Gunnery Lieutenant in the Gunnery Control Tower. And when Chief Petty Officer O'Flaherty pressed the trigger of the director, the little "bridges" in the ignition tubes heated up, the tubes took fire, the detonators at their ends exploded into the cordite charges, the cordite exploded, and the guns went off in a smashing madness of sound, like a clap of thunder confined in a small room. The solid charges of cordite changed themselves into vast masses of heated gas, so much gas that if expanded at that temperature it would form a volume more than equal to that of the five-thousand-ton ship itself, but confined at the moment of firing into a bulk no bigger than a large loaf of bread under a pressure a hundred times as great as the heaviest pressure in any ship's boiler. The pressure thrust itself against the bases of the shells, forcing them up the twenty-five-foot guns, faster and faster and faster. The lands of the rifling took hold of the driving bands of the shells—that rifling was of the finest steel, for the pressure against the sides of the lands, as the shells inertly resisted rotation, was as powerful as that of a hydraulic press. Up the guns went the shells, faster and faster forward, and spinning faster and faster on their axes, until when they reached the muzzles, twenty-five feet from the breech, they were rushing through the air at four times the speed of sound, having each acquired during that brief twenty-five feet an energy equal to that of a locomotive engine travelling at thirty miles an hour. And the recoil was exactly of the same amount of energy, as if each turret had been struck simultaneously by two locomotives moving at thirty miles an hour; but these two enormous blows fell merely on the recoiling systems of the guns—those recoiling systems over which so many ingenious brains had laboured, which represented the labour of so many skilled workmen, and which B turret crew had kept in high condition through years of warfare. Unseen and unfelt the hydraulic tubes of the recoil systems absorbed those two tremendous shocks; all that could be seen of their activity was the guns sliding slowly back and forward again. The two locomotives had been stopped in two seconds, as quietly as a woman might lean back against a cushion.[11]

If the book has any imperfections, they lie in the stereotypical, pusilanimous Italian admiral and his self-serving German advisor. The British seamen, on the other hand, are highly individualized. The naval action is fully plausible. In writing *The Ship*, besides serving the Allied cause, Forester created a robust, exciting, very masculine adventure story which foreshadows Forester's later and even more successful World War II naval books: *The Good Shepherd* (1955) and *Hunting the Bismarck* (1959).

The immediate prewar years and the war years mark Forester's achievement of full maturity as a novelist. It was an incredibly active period for him. He traveled widely from Hollywood to Britain, to Spain, and to Czechoslovakia. He wrote articles. He sailed on merchant ships and warships. He began the Hornblower Saga. He achieved full international recognition and fame as a writer. And he wrote three additional imaginative novels which brought him almost invariably favorable reviews, personal satisfaction, a sense of reaching variety, and considerable monetary remuneration.

CHAPTER 6

Postwar Allegory and Philosophy: 1947–1954

AS a world-renowned popular novelist with a following in the millions, and with his Hornblower novels serialized in the *Saturday Evening Post*, the most widely read family magazine in America, Forester could have stuck to the Hornblower Saga and continued to make a great deal of money and satisfy his readership without writing anything else. Instead, while producing three Hornblower novels in the 1947–1954 period, Forester wrote his two most philosophical novels: *The Sky and the Forest* (1948) and *Randall and the River of Time* (1950). He also published a book for adolescents—*The Barbary Pirates (1953)*—and under the title of *The Nightmare* (1954), a collection of short stories, of mixed quality, previously published in periodicals and all taking place during World War II.

The Sky and the Forest and *Randall and the River of Time* stand as fine achievements of a mature novelist who can work successfully in another genre besides the historical novel. It was time for Forester, more directly than ever before, to express his views on the inherent nature of man and the individual human being's relationship to time and the great historical events. *The Sky and the Forest* and *Randall and the River of Time* are very different novels in setting, intention, and scope; they bear witness to Forester's versatility, especially when one considers that they were written at the same time as *Mr. Midshipman Hornblower*, *Lieutenant Hornblower*, and *Hornblower and the Atropos*.

I *Africa Revisited*

With *The Sky and the Forest*, Forester returns to Central Africa, the scene of *The African Queen*. Instead of an Adam-Eve allegory set against a landscape improbably devoid of almost all other human inhabitants, this time Forester chose to allegorize the human condition in terms of man's cruelty, greed, and lust for power, in a jungle teeming with human and animal life to be harvested and spent by slavers and colonizers, where human life is the easiest and best source of animal protein for human consumption, and where people are fatted for slaughter. As in *The African Queen*, nature is also an adversary, but whereas in *The African Queen* the jungle is conquered by the blind determination of Rose and Charlie, in *The Sky and the Forest* nature wins by imposing its savage Darwinian Determinism on both "civilized" and "primitive" men as they make their initial contacts with one another. Perhaps the intervention of World War II between the writing of the two African novels and the coming of the Nuclear Age darkened Forester's view of the human potential to both endure adversity and preserve humanity, integrity, conscience, and love. If *The African Queen* is a book about hope, *The Sky and the Forest* is a triumph of despair.

The time is the mid-nineteenth century, when the African slave trade, having reached its peak, is beginning to decline and is primarily in the hands of Arabs from the North. Simultaneously the mysteries of the steaming jungle of Equatorial Africa were unfolding to European explorers and exploiters. In probing the savage mind, Forester selects a jungle king-god, who rules a village situated near a great river. He has total power over his village, its clearing, and the nearby river bank. Although only twenty-five years old, Loa has more than forty wives, the first of whom is Musini, with whom he has had his eldest child, his son Lanu, who is about ten years old when the story begins.

Initially, due to the nature of the forest and the heavy hand of tradition, Loa's rule is limited and lethargic. It encompasses a small population and a square mile or two of clearings, village, river bank, and jungle. It is a domain shared with pigmies who look upon Loa's people as food, and they are similarly perceived by their antagonists.

As a god, Loa relates to his brother, Sun, and his sister, Moon. The latter is coaxed back into the sky by appropriate ritual at monthly intervals. The people live, except for a very occasional ritual human slaughter for fresh meat, peacefully and indolently as their ancestors had for untold centuries, until Arabs and their black mercenaries arrive to capture slaves and steal ivory. The invaders have guns and an efficient organization. The village is destroyed, the old and very young are murdered, and the able-bodied are chained and whipped into submission. Loa, one moment a god, is suddenly less than human, a yoked, beaten slave being marched through the jungle into servitude.

However, Musini and Lanu escaped the slave raid and follow the slave march in order to effect an escape for Loa, too. Their loyalty to him represents an advance in human nature, for *The Sky and the Forest* is a book about change: change in the interpersonal relationships of members of a tribal community which had remained unchanged for centuries; change in the political aspect of African intertribal relations; and change in the economics of colonialism from the relatively inefficient Arab skimming of slaves and ivory to the highly technological European approach to black Africa as a place to be exploited over the long term for cash crops and ores. Forester knew his African history:

> For a thousand years at least, perhaps for many thousand years, the forest and its people had lain in torpor and peace. There had been food for all who could survive disease and cannibalism; there had been room enough for all, there had been materials enough to satisfy every simple need, and there had been no urge, either economic or temperamental, to wander or to expand. There prevailed an equilibrium which was long enduring even though it bore within itself the potentialities of instability, and it was the Arab invasions, pushing southwards from the fringes of the Sahara, westwards from the valley of the Nile and from the coast opposite Zanzibar, which first destroyed the equilibrium of the life in the deep central recess of the forest. On the Atlantic coast, where the great rivers met the sea, the disturbance began somewhat earlier as a result of the activities of Europeans. Hawkins on the Guinea Coast first bought from local chieftains the victims who otherwise would have gone to serve the chieftain's ancestors, and sold them at a vast profit on the other side of the Atlantic. More slaves, and more white men arrived, seeking gold and ivory and slaves, and willing to pay for them with commodities of inestimable desirability like spirits and brass and gunpowder; and the demand raised a turmoil far inland, for where local supplies were exhausted the local chiefs soon learned to make expeditions into the interior in search of more. Soon there was no more gold; the supply of ivory died away to the annual production when the accumulated reserves of ages were dissipated; but the forest still bred slaves, and slaves were sought at the cost of the ruin and the depopulation of the coastal belt.

> But no effect was evident in the deep interior of the forest. The cataracts on all the rivers, where they fall from the central plateau, the vast extent of the forest, and, above all, the desolation of the intermediate zone, hind-

ered for a long time the penetration of the deep interior either by the native chiefs of the coastal fringe or their white accomplices. The Napoleonic wars delayed the inevitable penetration, and when they ended the diminution and eventual suppression of the slave trade delayed it yet again. Towards the coast the strains and stresses of the slave-raiding wars had brought about the formation of powerful kingdoms—especially in the areas whither Mohammedan influence had penetrated form the Sahara—which subsequently had to be destroyed by the Europeans to gain for themselves free passage beyond them. The Hausa empire, Dahomey, Ashanti, and innumerable other native states, rose and later fell, built upon a foundation of barbarism cemented by European and Moslem influences. In the same way the intrusion of the Arabs from the east set the central part of the forest in a turmoil, so that war raged and no man's life was safe in his own town; and these developments occurred at the moment when Arab influence ebbed away as a result of events elsewhere, leaving the central forest disturbed and yet not further disturbed; as if the highest wave had swept the beach and none of its successors ever reached as high.[1]

Loa, Musini, and Lanu embark on an epic journey through the jungle to return to what is left of their village. The trip is fraught with dangers and new experiences and Loa is tempered, like the iron in his ax, from a dull, unthinking savage to a highly intelligent and calculating leader able to reorganize his village and to conquer much of the territory around him so that he creates a near-empire only to be thwarted by the cannon and rifles of the Europeans, which destroy his new kingdom and end his life and the lives of his wives and children:

. . . The rifle of the kneeling escort had followed Loa's movements, and the bullet struck Loa in the side as he poised on one foot with the ax above his head. From side to side the heavy bullet tore through him, from below upwards, expanding as it went. It struck below the ribs on his right side. It pierced his liver, it tore his heart to shreds, and, emerging, it shattered his left arm above the elbow. So Loa died in that very moment, the ax dropping behind him as he fell over with a crash. The rifleman tore open the breech, slid in another cartridge, and slammed the breechlock home. The skinny old woman saw Loa fall, and looked down at his body for one heartbroken moment. She uttered a shrill scream, and then raised her spider arms. It was as if she were going to attack . . . with her fingernails; perhaps that was in her mind, but there could be no certainty about it, for the rifleman pulled the trigger again, and the skinny old woman fell dying beside the body of her Lord.[2]

Loa represents the basic human potential for the organization of control over resources and collective society, fulfilled by adversity, cruelty, and natural selection. His growth and destruction are foreshadowed by Forester's example of the life and death of a clearing in the forest, struggled over by the elements of nature but doomed to return to the primal state:

> But where there was a clearing the scene changed. If a big tree paid the penalty for its very success by being selected to be struck by lightning, or if it had died of old age, or if a forest fire had killed trees over a larger area—and more especially where man had cut down trees for his own purposes—light and air could penetrate to earth level; and the lowly plants had their opportunity, which they grasped with feverish abandon. The clearing became a battleground of vegetation, a free-for-all wherein every green thing competed for the sunlight; until in a short time, measured in days rather than in weeks, the earth was covered shoulder-high by a tangle of vegetation through which no man could force his way without cutting a path with an ax or sword. For months, for years, the lowly plants had their way, dominating the clearing; but steadily the sapling trees forces their way through, to climb above and to pre-empt for themselves the vital light. It would be a long struggle, but as the years passed the trees would assert their mastery more and more forcibly; the undergrowth would die away, the fallen trees would rot to powder, and in the end the clearing would be indistinguishable from the rest of the forest, silent and dark.[3]

Loa is a learner. He learns that fish may be eaten, that baggage may be carried in canoes on the river, that fierce cruelty can keep a community in obedient terror, that power may be successfully delegated to trusted sons, and that through military strategy a leader may conquer and thrive, even bringing prosperity, peace, order, and a crude justice to an area. Always, however, in Forester's jungle-universe, there looms a Nemesis, another force building eventually to surplant the present order. Change is not only constant, it is accelerating.

Lastly, Loa is Forester's Everyman. He is vain, ignorant, selfish, cruel, superstitious, and lazy. Yet he can rise to noble stature in defense of his home; he can adapt to changing conditions of life; and he can recognize his own impermanence and mortality, meeting death with courage and dignity.

Forester's narrative skills continue to expand in *The Sky and the Forest*. The story is presented almost entirely through the eyes of Loa, and the reader quickly identifies with the primitive mind in the primal situation. As the savage mind is penetrated, the savage

continent is exposed. The tale rings with historical and anthropo-
logical authenticity while the vast forest is a fit cosmos for an allegory
of man. "The one note of disenchantment is near the end when
Forester, unaccountably, shifts his point of view from the world of
Loa to the world of the European invader. The reader's hypnosis
is snapped, but Forester's narrative sorcery is too assured even for
so abrupt an interruption to be fatal."[4]

Forester's study of the Congo must be compared to Joesph Conrad's much earlier *Heart of Darkness* (1899).[5] Both Forester and
Conrad set out to investigate the nature of evil. For both men, the
evil resulting from the loosening of civilization's restraints, as per-
sonified by Kurtz in *Heart of Darkness* and an English soldier of
fortune named Talbot in *The Sky and the Forest*, is worse than the
natural evil that stems from primitive ignorance, savagery, and need.
The latter is hardly evil at all, but merely a manifestation of the
struggle for survival. The civilized world should know better, but
in fact it is every bit as cruel and savage as the primitive world.
Indeed, its butchery is merely more efficient and sophisticated.
Without restraint Western man is the ultimate predator for both
Conrad and Forester. *Heart of Darkness* may focus more profoundly
on the mystery of human frailty and iniquity, but both books explore
and compare the dark realm of the nineteenth-century Congo and
the dark realm of the modern heart. Both *Heart of Darkness* and
The Sky and the Forest achieve poetic qualities: intensity, visual
and figurative metaphor, allegorical value, and profundity beyond
the literal scope of the language used.

II   *World War I Once More*

Randall and the River of Time (1950) is Forester's most philosophical novel. In it, Forester portrays collective human existence
manifestly as a flowing stream of history, with individual persons
caught up in the torrent, tossed about, shunted from mainstream
to eddy seemingly by chance, and always unaware that they have
no control over their own destinies. Metaphorically, history is a
series of currents composed of humanity and institutions such as the
army, the law, school, church, and family. It is ever changing. The
flotsam in the stream continually, like a kaleidoscope, change relationships, while time inexorably pulls everything and everyone
onward. Chance is both operative and inoperative. It is operative
because, from the human level of perception, chance encounters

and random choice determine one's position in the stream of life, even life or death; but yet there exists the possibility of a superior observation post from which a more discerning intelligence is able to see the patterns of flow that engulf human life and constitute human destiny.

Early in the novel, Forester indicates that the future of his hero, Charles Randall, depends not only upon chance but also the nature of his character which dictates his choices:

He was a peaceful little eddy of the great river at the moment. A floating fragment circling in an eddy may come out at some point of the circumference, and be hurried down the rapids to emerge in the pool below at a point quite different, and having followed a course quite different, from what would be the case if it emerged from the eddy at another place only an inch or two away. The whole subsequent course of that fragment may be profoundly affected by that small difference—by what appears to be the mere chance that dictates where it shall escape from the eddy. Naturally it is not mere chance. A mind possessed of enough knowledge and calculating ability could predict where the fragment would emerge from the eddy at the moment it entered. In the same way it was not mere chance that dictated Randall's future. That future hinged on whether, as he rose from the table, he should take Mrs. Speake in his arms or not, and that, in the same way, depended upon the sort of man Randall was, on what sort of upbringing he had had, what his previous experience had been, what tradition lay behind him.

If Randall had taken Mrs. Speake into his arms at that moment he would not have gone home that evening, probably not that night, and he would not have met Graham at his father's house, and his whole life would have been very different, so different that it is hard to imagine what would have happened to him. But the chances that had left Randall inexperienced, the chances that had made him that particular kind of man at that particular moment—and those chances are frightening in their complexity, even when no account is taken of those chances which had made Mrs. Speake just the woman she was at just that moment—all those chances dictated the present one.[6]

As in *The Sky and the Forest,* Forester's view of human destiny is highly deterministic. Randall, like Loa, is prisoner both of the limitations of his culture and the force of history of which he is a mere molecule in flux.

In *Randall and the River of Time,* Forester returns to earlier settings. As in *The General* and *The African Queen,* the time is World War I and immediately afterwards. As in so many of the early novels, most of the setting is in the London of Forester's youth.

The story begins in 1917. Charles Randall, son of a schoolmaster and member of a large middle-class family living in a London suburb, is nineteen and an infantry lieutenant in the British Army in France. His days seem numbered. Rather, one might think of his life in terms of minutes, not days, as the Western Front continues to take its ghastly toll of young life. Randall, interestingly enough, is just about the age Forester was in 1917 and he is fighting in the role Forester had the good fortune to miss and the perversity to regret.

Randall comes home on leave, where he meets a twenty-six-year-old married woman, Murial Speake, whose husband is a captain at the front. They almost have an affair, but Randall is too young and innocent to pursue Muriel, whom, anyway, he believes to be virtuous and true to her absent husband. She is, but less out of virtue than the fact that almost all able-bodied young men are at the front. He also meets, while on leave, a family friend named Graham who is in the business of securing patents for inventions. They talk about a military flare which has proved unsatisfactory in combat. Randall explains why and is coaxed by Graham into thinking of an improvement. Graham, a kindly old gentleman, who has lost both his sons in the war, takes a liking to Randall. The improvement is sold to the government and Randall is now an "inventor." Graham obtained for him a generous sum of money for his efforts. On the same leave, Randall and Muriel learn that Captain Speake has been killed. Randall, a naturally solicitous and decent youth, tries to help Muriel in her bereavement. Thus the leave from the front provides the "chance" that will prove to be both a source of financial success for Randall and a source of personal tragedy.

Returning to his battalion in France, Randall is called back to England to observe the tests of his improved flare. This chance saves him from the great German breakthrough of 1918, which wipes out his entire division. While in England, Muriel, who has been writing to him, realizes that he has a future as an inventor. She is a conniving, cynical woman who is entirely concerned for her own welfare. She manipulates Randall into proposing marriage to her and they are quickly married just before he leaves for the war again. Now a captain, he fortunately survives the last year of the conflict.

Demobilized, Randall seems an unattractive youth to the more experienced Muriel, who finds life with a university science student very dull. Unbeknownst to Randall, Muriel takes a lover, a one-legged ex–army captain named Massey. She becomes pregnant and leads Randall to believe that he is the father. Randall begins to work on a new invention for Graham and, coming home unexpectedly early one afternoon, finds Massey and Muriel in bed. There is confusion and Randall pushes Massey through a window to his death. Randall is charged with manslaughter and, after a lengthy and particularly well drawn trial scene, is acquitted despite Muriel's false and vicious testimony. Graham convinces Randall to leave for America to start a new life, and it seems apparent from the original dust jacket that Forester planned at least one sequel to the book, taking up Randall's story in the New World. Of course, he did not continue the story after all, one which might have been intended, from evidence in *Randall and the River of Time*, to chronicle Anglo-American life between the wars.

Randall and the River of Time is "a clear, well-managed story. . . ."[7] Randall is a likable innocent. He has been thrust into the mainstream of history at far too young an age and thus in his late teens he is trained to be a superb killer rather than educated to be an adjusted, contributing member of society. One of the most savage ironies of the book is that both Captain Randall and Captain Massey have killed dozens of men in war, yet when one almost accidentally kills the other, in a most clumsy and nearly comic manner, the entire society focuses on the event of the death of a naked, one-legged, ex-cricketer lover, ostensibly to see justice done, but really out of prurient interest. The system is sound. Randall is fairly acquitted. The institution of British law is part of the river of time and it runs true. The perspective of the novel is seen as if from an observation plane flying slowly over the movement of humanity, allowing the observer to sight and follow one specimen, typical yet individual, as indeed all human examples must be. Thus Randall is a fully developed, fully realized fictional protagonist, whereas one of the book's few weaknesses is that only Randall is a complete character. All other persons in the work have elements of caricature: the barrister in wig, the gruff general, the ineffectual schoolmaster father, and so on. Muriel comes closer to realization but she is made so mean and grasping by nature and circumstance that ultimately there is little that either Forester or the reader can do with her.

The anonymous reviewer in the *Times Literary Supplement* faulted Forester for not emphasizing the psychological aspect of Randall and Muriel's relationship.[8] He missed the point. There is no such relationship between them. She, an experienced woman, married for security and out of a maternal interest in a handsome boy in uniform seemingly about to die in combat. He was her pawn, her victim. After his return to civilian life and the drabness of ill-fitting civilian clothes, they ceased to have anything to talk about. She could even carry on a love affair under Randall's unseeing eyes and within earshot of the undistracted student. Randall in the tragedy of his generation has not been educated to think but trained to obey orders. He can be an inventor cleverly carrying out Graham's request to invent a pea sorter, but never a scientist working inductively and creatively.

Forester remains the master of battle description. Early in the book he paints a scene of a German raid on a British trench position:

It was still dark, and the rain was falling briskly. A duckboard reared up under his foot so that he slipped into the detestable mud; he recovered himself with a curse and stumbled on to identify himself when challenged as he entered the bay. And then it happened—the appalling noise, the vivid flashes, shouts in the darkness, the sharp crashing explosions of grenades—subsequent ones muffled, indicating that bombs were going off after being pitched into a dugout. Rifleshots; machine guns raving, flares going up all along the line. It was only a matter of seconds before the artillery caught the alarm as the gunners ran to their guns; up and down the line could be heard the din as if a thousand doors were being slammed, and shells were flying overhead and bursting in volcanoes of mud. The Germans had raided No. 11 post. That much was evident instantly. No one could tell at the moment whether it was the beginning of a general attack or not, which was why the flares were going up, and why nervous machine gunners were traversing their fire back and forth along the line. Before the question could be decided Randall and the company commander were gathering men for a counter-attack, Randall shaking off his sleepy stupidity as he listened to his captain's orders bellowed through the din; his heart was pounding with excitement as he looked round him in the light of the flares at the mud-daubed men crowding into the bay. Then he started off down the trench, revolver in hand, bayonet man and bomber preceding him, back to the junction, up the other communication trench. The din was still going on up and down the line, shaking the earth; but ahead of them, as they went round one traverse and another, there was silence. Not silence round the next bend; groans. Dead men and wounded men, lying in the bottom of the trench, and fainter groans, a chorus of faint groans, coming up from the mouth of the dugout beyond. A flare which went up near enough to light their path—paler than usual in the growing light—showed them a dead German lying with his face on the firing step, and the raindrops glistened in the flare as they fell. There were only dead and wounded in the post; the garrison had been wiped out.[9]

In his power to depict World War I battle scenes Forester here as in *The General* rivals the abilities of such World War I writers as Robert Graves, Erich Maria Remarque, and Siegfried Sassoon, men who, unlike Forester, had been in battle. Captain Randall, now all of twenty years old, is an excellent company commander. Forester shows us the final breakthrough of the war through the eyes of this battle hardened veteran:

Excited men, tired men, untrained men, paid little attention to the orders; falling on their stomachs they opened fire without adjusting their sights and emptied their magazines as fast as they could work bolt and trigger. Even the Lewis guns' better-trained crews were carried away with excitement, while the conditions for taking aim, with the valley dropping away below them, were difficult. All the lead that went winging across the valley seemed to be misdirected. The battery struggled on while from the willows by the stream came the slower beat of German machine guns and the air above Randall's head was filled with the shriek of bullets. The Lewis gun beside Randall jammed, and the cursing gunner trying to clear the jam fell forward shot through the chest. Randall left it to run to where a dozen riflemen without an officer were lying firing wildly across the valley. He plumped down among them; the furrow in which they lay gave excellent cover.

"Cease fire, men!" he said, twisting his neck left and to right and repeating his words until he won obedience.

"Get your sights for nine hundred yards. Make sure of that, now. You, Winter—that's not nine hundred on your sights. That's better. Now reload, all of you. Now take careful aim at that battery. When I say 'Fire!' start shooting, slowly. Make sure you take aim for every shot. Now, everyone ready? Fire!"

It was death that the rifles began to spit now across the valley—most of them at least. Randall saw that Private Jones was hopeless as a marksman.

"Give me your rifle, Jones."

Randall aimed carefully, squeezed the trigger, aimed and fired again. Men and horses across the valley were dropping; one gun, its team presumably disorganized by a wounded horse, swung clear round. A Lewis gun crew managed to steady themselves long enough to put in a long and accurate burst, so that horses and men fell like wheat under a scythe. Now everyone was paying stricter attention to his duty. Now the battery was wiped out. Every man and every horse was dead, and the guns stood helpless on the hillside. Now that that target had been satisfactorily disposed of attention could be paid to the covering rear guard down in the willows, and plans made for rooting them out. But over there on the left there were British troops already across the stream; with their flank turned those fellows must retreat or die or surrender. There goes one lot making a dash for it. Don't let them get away! See them all fall, caught in a machine-gun burst—

that last one lying on his belly with his short legs kicking. There's another one! Get 'im! Hold your fire, here's one lot surrendering. My God! Did you see that? The group that had made its appearance, coming forward with its hands up, had been caught in a blast from another German machine gun, every man falling dead, rightful victims of their fellow countrymen's wrath. That meant that the other guns down there would fight it out to the last.

"Sergeant Thwaites, see if you can get your section along down that gully there. Hibberd! They've got one gun in the bend right ahead, one finger left of that white tree. Give 'em a long burst. Come on, man, we don't want to be here all day."[10]

In *The General* Forester implied the mindlessness of the brutality of World War I and the possiblity that the war was avoidable and all in vain. In *Randall and the River of Time,* Forester states his unmitigated revulsion for the war that took the lives of most of his comrades and practically destroyed the civilization in which he had grown up:

Heretics had been tortured by the Inquisition; red men had devised methods of making their captives scream in agony. In the years to come the Nazis were to try to outdo these achievements in the cruelties of their prison camps. A furious and desperate war was to open twenty-one years after the close of its predecessor, with slaughter and heroism and misery. But at no time in the history of misery was there such suffering as a purely fortuitous combination of circumstances brought to a million human beings in 1917. The Marquis de Sade might dream of tortures, but not his insane imagination could compass the torments which chance dealt out to the devoted infantry of the nations at war. For a special reason the freezing dungeons of the Inquisition, the iron cages of Louis XI, were not to be compared with the wet and the cold and the slime of the water-logged trenches in Flanders, where men stood night and day knee-deep in icy mud, or took their rest, head bowed, sitting on a firing step hardly more solid. There was a reason why the degradation of Buchenwald was not as deep as the degradation of the brutish filth of the Salient.

For the men who fought in those trenches had the additional torment of the suspicion that remedy lay in their own hands, that if only they could think of the right way to deal with the problem they could nullify the stupidity of the peoples and the generals who were driving them to hideous death. It was not by the easy method of self-murder, and it would be something less obvious than mass mutiny, although allied to it. They were in the grip of something implacable and yet not necessarily inevitable; in the disillusionment of 1917 they feared that they were giving up their lives, their sanity, and their dignity for something which later on, when they were all mad, crippled, or dead, would be found to be nothing; it was this feeling that doubled their regrets and halved their infantile pleasures.[11]

In the end, however, the forces of history are as inevitable and irresistible as a great flood. Randall and all men and women are rushed along to their individual destinies, a molecular part of the collective destiny of a people in their own time:

The river of time was whirling him along. Chance eddies had flung him here; chance eddies had flung him there. The broad river had a myriad of channels, and now an eddy was parting him from the other flotsam with which he had been circling and was pushing him far over into another channel altogether. There he might circle, there he might come into contact with other flotsam, but always he would be hurried along, down the smooth reaches, over the cataracts, until at last he would be cast ashore and the river would hurry along without him.[12]

The *Times Literary Supplement* reviewer's ultimate comment on *Randall and the River of Time* was that "it is difficult to avoid the feeling that Mr. Forester is more at home with Captain Hornblower."[13] He was wrong again. Forester was much more "at home" with Randall, who could have been a companion of his youth, who indeed could, except for "chance," have been Forester himself.

During the 1947–1954 period, Forester achieved the high point of his fame, a pinnacle he would hold until his death in 1966. His Hornblower was a household name. All his other works were continually compared to the Hornblower books. Everywhere Forester went, his own name was recognized until he and his wife had to travel incognito to avoid autograph-seekers. He made a great deal of money and now was quite comfortably set for life. He was turning out about one book per year with a waiting audience in the millions looking forward to serialization of the Hornblower Saga as Charles Dickens's readers had done a century before and the same millions awaiting the bound copies of his various novels. Yet it was in this period of his life and work that Forester, now quite aware of the frailty of his health, turned to more philosophical writing in *The Sky and the Forest* and *Randall and the River of Time*. After this period Forester would devote the remainder of his literary career to Hornblower, to history, and to action writing. Philosophy, *Weltanschauung*, and deeper thought were abandoned, perhaps because Forester felt ill-suited to the role of philosophical novelist, perhaps because althouth the reviews were generally quite favorable for *The*

Sky and the Forest and *Randall and the River of Time*, the critics, except for the British who were rather negative, did not treat these books as seriously as Forester probably felt they should have and both American and British reviewers constantly compared the non-Hornblower novels to the Saga. It was an unfair if understandable practice. They were simply unable to see Forester in any role except that of historical novelist.

Forester's philosophical novels are not great works of literature. He wrote them as a middle-aged man who had seen, understood, and written about much war and economic upheaval, and he wrote them after a lifelong study of history. His thought and his work led him to a philosophy of history that was partially historical determinism, partly economic determinism, and partly natural selection. Loa, representing primitive man, and Randall representing modern civilized man, are both presented as chess pieces in the great, unending game of human destiny referred to retrospectively as history. They feel from time to time that they have the power of decision, but in reality the choices they make are predetermined by their culture, their character, and their history. Furthermore, at any given time in their brief lives, great forces are at work such as Colonialism, Imperialism, Fascism, Communism, Evangelical Christianity, and many others. They roll over mankind. They overlap and interlace. Men and women, great and small, are caught in the currents of history, never fully realizing what is happening to them.

It's a pessimistic philosophy. The only optimistic note is that from time to time men and women rise above circumstance, as if they were thrusting head and shoulders out of the river for a brief moment, to perform acts of courage or generosity or intelligence or creativity or love. These acts are surprising because they occur so seldom and are so difficult to do. If life on the surface was very rich for Forester in this period of his work, his mind, nevertheless, was dwelling on the darker side of human experience. Life for Forester was merely a part of the continuum of the existence of the universe. It was not, however, progressive, and the future would seem to offer little hope that mankind would be able to deal more successfully with his ever more complex environment than he dealt with his simpler immediate or remote past.

CHAPTER 7

Last Works: 1955–1966

DURING the final phase of his writing career, Forester wrote only one non-Hornblower novel, *The Good Shepherd* (1955), a book he had begun back in World War II. A collection of his World War II stories, entitled *The Man in the Yellow Raft* (1969), as mediocre as *The Nightmare* (1954), was published posthumously. His main attention was divided between the Hornblower Saga, for which he wrote *Hornblower in the West Indies* (1958), *Hornblower and the Hotspur* (1962), *The Hornblower Companion* (1964), and the unfinished *Hornblower during the Crisis* (published 1967); and naval history. In the latter genre Forester produced his most serious historical work, *The Age of Fighting Sail: The Story of the Naval War of 1812* (1956; published in London as *The Naval War of 1812*, 1957), and the exciting recreation of the search for the elusive World War II German battleship *Bismarck*, *Hunting the Bismarck* (1959; American title: *The Last Nine Days of the Bismarck*). It appears that Forester had decided to devote the remainder of his creative life to completing the Hornblower Saga and to investigating special topics in naval history. The last non-Hornblower novel, however, is one of Forester's finest pieces of fiction.

I On Convoy Duty Once More

The Ship depicted cruiser action on British convoy duty in the Mediterranean Sea during World War II. It emphasized heroic combat on a stout ship with the vessel essentially the protagonist of the story. *The Good Shepherd*, written some twelve years afterwards, is the story of Allied North Atlantic convoy duty; it is much less "fictional" and heroic; and, most importantly, the emphasis is not upon a ship, but upon a human protagonist, Commander George Krause, United States Navy.

The Good Shepherd is a first-rate novel about World War II. It provides Forester with yet another opportunity to explore the possibility of independent command under stress, a Hornblower situation indeed. Because of the solitude of his command situation and his self-doubting and critical yet resolute nature, Commander Krause is Forester's last and perhaps finest single example of the Man Alone. His adventure and trial as a convoy commander in the North Atlantic in 1943 are set against the background of Forester's most vivid writing about World War II at sea, a background that draws the reader into the book with a sense of participation that is even more real than the action scenes in the best of Hornblower.

The Good Shepherd is the stirring account of a mere forty-eight hours in the desperate life of a North Atlantic convoy at the time when the tide was running for the German submarines in their fierce wolf packs. Commander Krause is charged with seeing that his convoy of thirty-seven poky merchantmen gets through to help supply starving Britain. His escort squadron is completely inadequate for the task. Instead of a dozen destroyers needed to protect the convoy adequately, he has only four warships at his command: his own destroyer, the U.S.S. *Keeling*, a Polish destroyer, and two tiny corvettes, one British and one Canadian, all of which make for a nice ethnic, Allied mix.

Krause (his German name is one of the ironies of the book) is the good shepherd tending his flock; a biblical shepherding through the valley of watery death is the central metaphor of the novel. He is not a brilliant man, nor, despite his twenty-odd years in the navy, has he ever seen action before. He is taciturn. In fact the novel is nearly devoid of conversation. Almost all of the actual dialogue consists of commands and orders to the helm or comments on the submarine actions. Krause has been passed over for promotion in the peacetime navy. Only war could have brought him to the rank of commander and his present independent command. He has little hope for further success in rank, but never for one moment does he doubt that he will bring most of the convoy safely to still waters. His brief marriage was a failure, partly because he was so devoted to duty, partly because of his old-fashioned religious nature, all of which were difficult for his wife to understand, and so she became involved with a San Francisco attorney and divorced Krause.

There is little else remaining to Krause except his acute sense of duty. It is to his concept of duty that the commander is wed, and that is his tragedy and his glory. He will bring the convoy through

despite his own inexperience, despite the loss of seven merchantmen, despite the sinking of the Polish destroyer, precisely because
it is his duty to do so. The losses are acceptable in the desperate
hours of the war at sea, and two, possibly three U-Boats are destroyed in the process. At Annapolis, Krause was an Olympic fencer
and thus he is able reflexively to thrust at and parry with the hidden
enemy, anticipating moves with increasing success. The story is
more his story than the convoy's: his anxiety, his suffering, his
exhaustion, his inner strength, his toughness, his personal bitter-
ness, and his religious heart and believing soul. Krause, the son of
a Lutheran parson, kneels in prayer before sleeping and believes
both in God and Man. Thus, as though stemming from his thoughts,
the book is laced with biblical quotations, through which Forester
as author and Krause as protagonist link thoughts. It is a brilliant
structural idea. For example, as Krause is surveying the domain of
his convoy, they think: "An outlying ship like that would be a choice
victim, to be torpedoed without any chance of one of the escort
running down to the attack at all. Be sober, be vigilant; because
your adversary the devil, as a roaring lion, walketh about, seeking
whom he may devour."[1]

The biblical references are not separate paragraphs, or reflections
by Krause in various situations. They are a means through which
the narrator forges the closest possible identification with the hero
without writing the book in the first person. Consequently, the
reader too is able to empathize quickly, closely, and fully with
Krause, who is the only developed character in the novel. The form
of the novel is not a first-person monologue, or an interior dialogue,
but something of a conversation between omniscient author and a
strong hero, with the former narrating the background and creating
the events, while the latter reacts to the events, reveals his thoughts,
and pursues an action. The Bible and the good-shepherd metaphor
are the meeting ground of their respective experiences and the
artery through which characterization is transfused from Forester
to Krause.

When the convoy commander (Krause is the escort commander,
responsible for the convoy's safety) signals to the *Keeling*, the
Krause-Forester persona reflects: "Comconvoy had to word his signal like that, persumably; he was making requests of an associate,
not giving orders to a subordinate. Let thy words be few, said
Ecclesiastes; the officer drafting an order had to bear that recom-
mendation in mind, but a retread admiral addressing an escort com-

mander had to remember the Pslams and make his words smoother than butter."[2] And when Krause signals they mutually reflect: "I say to this man, Go, and he goeth; and to another, Come, and he cometh. But what of the 'great faith' that centurion had? *Dodge* was already wheeling round to carry out her orders."[3]

The biblical quotations pervade, flavor, and structure the novel, and along with the fact that the story transpires in a forty-eight-hour period marked not by chapters but by the changing of the traditional four-hour navy watches, they help create an extremely tight work of art that may be described fairly as dramatically classical: adhering to the unities of time, place, and action, while using the common religious text for symbol and allegory.

When Krause is maneuvering his escorts in pursuit of the U-boats, the narrative again combines biblical past and historical present through the fused persona: "That tremendous temptation again to call for flank speed, and chance muffling the sonar; the temptation must be put aside. Blessed is the man that endureth temptation; for when he is tried, he shall receive the crown of life. On this course they would pass clear by a wide margin of the area of tortured water. . . ."[4]

There are several other examples of this device in *The Good Shepherd*. Forester probably could not have used this technique in a book that did not have a deeply religious hero, or in a work not involved with an individual human being's life-and-death struggle, enlarged to titanic proportions by powerful machines of death, vast stretches of sea, and hundreds of involved lives. For *The Good Shepherd* the idea was very good indeed.

Forester developed a particularly acute method of setting off the major actions of war by focusing from time to time on the needs or thoughts or movements of individual humans, as if to remind us subconsciously that the tapestry of war is woven, first of all, with human strands, and even men in mortal combat must eat, and sleep, and move their bowels. Krause sometimes suffers physical pain simply because he cannot find a minute in the passing hours of war to urinate. He is a coffee addict, perhaps his only weakness or indulgence. In a bold stroke of characterization, Forester stops the battle momentarily to deal with Krause and coffee, thus permanently establishing his warrior-chieftain-protagonist's humanity:

There was just light enough to see the Filipino mess boy in his white coat. In his hands was a tray covered with a white napkin, as he had been taught to serve meals, and as he always would serve them, with U-boats on the horizon or not. He had obviously just tried to put the tray down on the pilothouse chart table, and had as obviously been shooed away by the indignant quartermaster in jealous charge of the chart and instruments there. Now he stood unhappily holding it, swinging with the heel of the ship; Krause knew exactly how, under the napkin, the cream—they still brought him up cream although they ought by now to know he never used it—and coffee were slopped over the tray cloth. And worse might happen at any moment. The tray soared up and swooped down in the half darkness as *Keeling* rose over a wave. Krause suddenly felt he could not bear the thought of that precious load falling to the deck. He grabbed at pot and cup, balanced himself, and poured the cup half full. He balanced again, pot in one hand, cup in the other. In that second there was nothing in the whole world that he wanted as much as that coffee. His mouth was dry even though his face was still wet. He sipped thirstily at the scalding stuff, sipped again, and drained the cup. He could feel the comforting fire of it all the way down his throat. He smacked his lips like a savage, poured himself another half cup, and, watching his moment, set the pot on the tray.

"Put that tray on the deck and don't take your eye off it," he said.

"Aye aye, sir."

He drank again. It was only nine hours since he had breakfasted, but he did not think a man could possibly feel so thirsty or so hungry. The thought of pouring unlimited coffee into himself, and then of eating to ease his savage hunger, filled him with exultation.[5]

The Good Shepherd is almost as much a book about duty as it is about war. The most salient feature in the makeup of Commander George Krause is his deep-seated sense of duty which stems from his religious Protestant background and his single-minded love for the navy. Duty begins with God and extends to the Good Cause through the medium of his ship:

The pleasure was not even spoiled when a sudden recollection came to him of a duty yet unfulfilled. He bowed his head for a moment.

"I thank Thee, O Lord, for all Thy mercies—"[6]

In the agony of sleep-deprived fatigue, duty continually brings him, almost masochistically, back to battery:

There was absolutely no excuse for him to nod off. But now he had had his warning. He had discovered the insidiousness of the enemy he had to fight against. He would never let it happen again. He got down from the stool and stood erect. The protests of his leg muscles would keep him awake;

and his feet were painful now that he stood on them. It really seemed as if his shoes were far too tight for him, as if his feet had grown a size larger during the night. He thought for a moment of taking off his shoes—old and tried companions though they were—and sending down for the slippers in his cabin. But the idea only grew up in his mind to be cut down again instantly. A captain had an example to set and should never appear at his post of duty in slippers; and self-indulgence whether physical or moral was something treacherous and rightly suspect—he had had a clear example of that just now when he fell asleep on his stool. And—and—perhaps if he stood long enough his feet would go numb and cease to hurt him so.[7]

Duty in the just cause of the defense of democracy is what Forester envisions as mankind's hope. Western civilization based on Judeo-Christian ethics will continue to produce men and women who, although in most ways are ordinary mortals with average intelligence and creativity, will rise to the demanding occasion of a moral crisis and will not be found wanting by their fellow human beings. This sense of hope and belief in such works as *The Ship*, *The Good Shepherd*, and even *Hunting the Bismarck* is one of the most pleasing, satisfying, and comforting aspects of Forester's work.

In the end the just man goes on. The chance-destiny enigma which Forester formulated in *Randall and the River of Time* is still operative in the author's cosmos:

There was still duty to be done and life to be lived; and it did not clash with duty to ask BuPers for assignment in the Atlantic seaboard, away from Southern California and the house in Coronado; to tear off the fragile roots that had begun to sprout; to face the rest of life with duty as his sole companion. Chance—the chance that elevated a paranoiac to supreme power in Germany and a military clique to power in Japan—dictated that when it was too late he should receive the coveted promotion to commander, if it can be called chance. Chance had made him an orphan; chance had brought about the senator's nomination. Chance had put him in command of the convoy escort. Chance had made him the man he was and had given that man the duty he had to carry out.

Now he was asleep. He could be called happy now, lying spreadeagled and face downward on his bunk, utterly unconscious.[8]

There is rest to be had by the just man serving the just cause, especially one who has served in solitary command, and has met the supreme challenge of the Man Alone. Krause is Forester's ultimate hero: he endured and he succeeded.

The Good Shepherd rivals the best of Hornblower in providing reader satisfaction with a good story, a clear vision of right and wrong, a strong central character, and a precise, accurate depiction of significant naval action. ". . . in Forester's chosen field, and when his talents for creating a sense of participation and of identification are in top gear, he has no master and few peers. As the convoy reaches safety, as Krause sinks down on his bunk in stunned sleep, you could well say this is the way it was in the North Atlantic in the bad time. And you would be right."9

II 1812

In *The Age of Fighting Sail*, C. S. Forester, writing for the Mainstream of America Series, combined good history and good narrative. It is a felicitous book because it presented Forester with an opportunity to do everything he did best as a writer: describe naval life and combat in the Age of Sail, deal with seapower and maritime strategy, and write history of the Napoleonic period. Not surprisingly, therefore, the Duke of Wellington, a general, of course, serving in Spain, then France, and then Vienna, is nevertheless a major figure in *The Age of Fighting Sail*. Also, not surprisingly, Forester elevated the fierce single ship actions in the war as well as the few small fleet encounters into an epic drama, for the subject allowed him to exercise real-life naval heroes in his favorite philosophical maneuver: the Man Alone. That almost all the heroes of the book are Americans is surely not due to any bias on Forester's part, but rather to the fact that the Americans were impossibly outnumbered: thirteen warships against over eight hundred.

Forester points out that President James Madison ill-advisedly dragged a divided country into war with the world's greatest sea power, Great Britain, in 1812. Although the city of Washington was burned, the coastal areas of the United States ravished, the American invasion of Canada ended in failure, New England prepared for secession, all American ports were blockaded, nevertheless the United States of America emerged from the War of 1812 more united than when they had entered it. Forester implies that this development was due almost entirely to the single-ship victories of the United States Navy over the supposedly invincible Royal Navy and the strategic victories in the battles of Lake Erie and Champlain which prevented a British counterinvasion. The only other factor in producing the emerging American consciousness was General Andrew Jackson's victory at the Battle of New Orleans, which, in fact, occurred after the peace treaty had been signed but before the news could reach the southern city.

Forester strongly and correctly argues that the war did not result in a combat victory for the United States. Thus Forester "restored reality to the War of 1812."[10] Madison sent the nation into war (while Great Britain was engaged in a desperate struggle with Napoleon) to secure free trade and abolish the British practice of impressing American seamen into the Royal Navy. Neither causes are mentioned in the peace treaty. As early as June 1814 Madison privately admitted defeat. However, the war did not end in an American surrender, because, as Wellington wisely pointed out, the United States simply did not offer enough concentrated military targets to permit a European-type conquest and occupation. Even if the major American cities like New York, Boston, and Philadelphia were occupied, the nation, as in the Revolutionary War, could fight a guerrilla war indefinitely. The War of 1812 ended because both parties found the continuation of the war no longer to be in their respective interests. The British were having trouble once more on the Continent and needed their battalions at Dover more than they needed them in Montreal. The United States posed no mortal threat to Britain; European powers did. America needed to end the war because the nation's economic losses were devastating and the maritime freedoms desired were not obtainable by force of arms.

So the War of 1812 accomplished nothing tangible for either side. However, in the end, for America there was "Old Ironsides," Andy Jackson, "The Star-Spangled Banner," "Don't Give Up the Ship," better-defined borders with Canada, growing international respect for American maritime power and rights, and the emergence of a victorious fighting tradition for the United States Navy, a tradition that has been carried down to the present day.

Forester relied heavily for his material on two previously published books: Theodore Roosevelt's *The Naval War of 1812* (1882) and Admiral Alfred Thayer Mahan's *Sea Power in Its Relations to the War of 1812* (1905). From Roosevelt he obtained many of the details of the ships' encounters. In Mahan he found a thematic concept which he continually implies in *The Age of Fighting Sail;* that is, the best hope for world peace lies in Anglo-American naval supremacy. Mahan also offered support for two other salient military themes in Forester's history, that American naval preparedness is vital for the defense of the Western world and that a military complacency resulting merely from superior numbers may lead to unexpected defeats similar to those that overtook the Royal Navy, long conqueror of the French, Dutch, Spanish, and Danish fleets, in its initial encounters with the big frigates of the fledgling American Navy.

The history's American title, *The Age of Fighting Sail*, is, of course, a misnomer. The age of fighting sail began in the early Middle Ages and lasted to the mid-nineteenth century. Forester's book deals only with the Anglo-American conflict from 1812 to 1815. The English title, *The Naval War of 1812*, is an accurate one, but Forester or his publisher may have felt constrained not to use the same title as Roosevelt's earlier book in the United States. Forester begins with a study of the American grievances which led to the declaration of war with Great Britain on June 18, 1812: the practice of Royal Navy impressment of seamen from American ships, the violation of the sovereignty of American territorial waters, and the blockading of the entire European continent to the exclusion of American trade.

Forester's old and favorite historical antagonists are present in the beginning:

The Grand Army had crossed the Nieman. The Imperial hordes, urged on by the Imperial freebooter, were pouring into Russia, destined for Moscow—and destined to retreat from Moscow, such of them as survived. And Wellington had crossed the Agueda, marching out of Portugal with an incomparable British army to free three quarters of Spain from French dominion and to strike the shattering blow of Salamanca that would cause the French military structure to totter on its foundations. It was all in the same week that Bonaparte crosssed the Nieman, that Wellington crossed the Agueda, and Mr. Madison crossed the Rubicon.[11]

However, the ultimate antagonists of *The Age of Fighting Sail* are President Madison and the Duke of Wellington, with the latter appearing to be the wiser, the more intelligent, and the more sensitive leader.

Forester then begins the saga of the great frigates, which were, of course, the cruisers, not the battleships of their day: the *Constitution*, the *President*, the *United States*, the *Chesapeake*, the *Essex*, and the *Constellation*. The gallant smaller American vessels, brigs and sloops, which were like contemporary destroyers, are also chronicled: the *Enterprise*, the *Hornet*, the *Peacock*, and the *Wasp*.

Forester's narrative, as he describes with relish the naval battles, is superb. "The author is dazzling in his display of sea lore, and authoritative in his understanding of sail warfare."[12] The *Hornet* meets the British *Peacock:*

Each ship had a main battery of carronades, there could be no question of maneuvering at long range. They rushed at each other; the *Hornet* managed to gain the weather gauge and the ships exchanged broadsides, passing on opposite tacks. Peake wore the *Peacock* round, perhaps with the idea of crossing his opponent's stern, but Lawrence was too quick for him and the *Hornet* too handy. The American, wheeling round over the blue sea in the flaming sunset, came up against the *Peacock's* quarter and shot her opponent to pieces in less than fifteen minutes. "Eggshells armed with hammers" was an expression employed in a later age to describe a very different class of ship, but it applied well enough to the present antagonists. The fragile sides of a gun brig could be torn to pieces in no time by the smashing fire of heavy carronades at close range.

That was exactly what happened to *Peacock.* She was reduced to a sinking condition while her masts still stood. Almost one third of her crew were killed or wounded, her captain being killed. Her first lieutenant hailed to say she had surrendered; water was pouring in fast through her shattered sides and she sent up a distress signal immediately after. The prize crew sent on board tried to save her; they anchored (one mast went over the side at that moment) and tried to plug the shot holes and heave the guns overside, but she sank so rapidly that some men, both British and Americans, were trapped below and drowned. Sinking as she did on a comparatively even keel and in shoal water, her foremast head remained above water, and a lucky few saved themselves by racing up the shrouds ahead of the pursuing water; the rest found themselves afloat in the shattered boat and on the wreckage that drifted off the booms.[13]

A particularly effective aspect of *The Age of Fighting Sail* is the manner in which the individual character of the various American captains is expressed. To a considerable extent, Forester is fascinated by them because, unlike their British counterparts, who were continually under the command of station admirals and ultimately of the British Admiralty, the Americans perforce operated on their own, making not only tactical but strategic and political decisions alone. In broad strokes, he sketches Commodore John Rodgers's cautious, intelligent grasp of national strategy; Captain James Lawrence's impetuosity and bad luck; Captain Isaac Hull's cool professionalism, Captain William Bainbridge's tactical skill; Captain David Porter's wide ranging imagination; and the irrepressible Captain Stephen Decatur's panache and verve.

The war to control the strategic inland seas, Lakes Ontario, Erie, and Champlain, receives particular attention from Forester, who realized, as did both the American and British governments, that the only remotely conceivable way the United States could be defeated was through spearheads reaching down from Canada to the East Coast of America, thus dividing the country; and the only leverage the Americans could obtain over the British, besides the depletion of her merchant marine through privateers, was by means of the threat of, or actual invasion of Canada. Neither objective could be obtained without naval control of the upper Great Lakes and Lake Champlain. Thus the truly significant strategic naval actions were the fleet actions on the lakes.

Forester devotes three key chapters to the war of the inland waters. The campaign on Lake Ontario resulted in a stalemate due for the most part to the overcautious nature of both the British and the American commanders. Long-term control of Ontario might have decided the war; American control meant control of Upper Canada, and British control meant the conquest of the American frontier and the end of American westward expansion.

The other lake wars, however, were decisive enough in their outcome to prevent the war from concluding with a major American military defeat. Forester reconstructs the Battle of Lake Erie and the Battle of Lake Champlain with tactical accuracy and painstaking concern for strategic implications. He also expressed his admiration for the American commanders, Commodore Oliver Hazard Perry and Lieutenant Thomas Macdonough, who not only were Men Alone making great strategic decisions far from the centers of political power but who also had to build their small fleets and man them in the wilderness. They were men much to Forester's liking and he recreates their characters, motivations, and actions with all the care of a consummate novelist.

Chance and destiny are juxtaposed once more in Forester's writing, so that the author sees both manifesting the outcome of battles and the war itself. Destiny was served when at long last both sides realized that their future best interest lay in parallel and not conflicting policy. Chance exerted influence tactically, as when the American frigate *Constitution* met the British frigate *Guerriere* in the first significant naval action of the war:

Then came the final coincidence. A month after running *Guerriere*'s topsails over the horizon at the end of the historic chase, Hull saw them coming up over the horizon again as she was making her way to Halifax in obedience to Broke's orders. Hull had made the rounds of Boston and Halifax and the St. Lawrence; Dacres had been far out in the Atlantic with Broke and the convoy. Both Broke and Hull had made the incorrect deductions, usual in wartime, from imperfect premises; both had acted on the soundest military principles, and this was the result, this entirely accidental meeting hundreds of miles from land.[14]

And chance affects the great strategic encounters, too:

The two American victories on the Lakes were due in very large part to the personal exertions of the American leaders. If Perry had fallen on the quarter-deck of the *Lawrence*—and the chances were about three to two that he did fall—the battle of Lake Erie might well have ended in a repulse for the American squadron, with the *Lawrence* left in British hands to carry with her superiority of force as soon as she could be patched up. If Macdonough had been killed by Downie's opening broadside—as were one fifth of his men while he himself was hurt—the *Saratoga* might not have fought so hard; she could certainly not have been handled more methodically. Downie was killed during the first few minutes. We learn little about him during his brief nine days of command, but we do know that before his death *Confiance's* fire was highly effective and that it fell away steeply after it. With Macdonough dead and Downie alive, the battle of Lake Champlain might have ended like some of the battles between the English and the Dutch, like Parker's Dogger Bank action, in a drawn battle with the two opponents too exhausted to fight on.[15]

The Age of Fighting Sail is Forester's finest effort in the sphere of nonfiction. It shows that, had he chosen, he could have been one of the century's major historiographers of the Napoleonic period. "This book deserves to stand beside Mahan's and Roosevelt's, for it delineates the role of the Naval War of 1812 in helping America discover its national identity. More suggestive in interpretation than its predecessors, it points to the unbreakable connections between a war's historical setting and the course of its conduct, between fighting men and their luck, and—not least of all—between good history and good narrative."[16]

III Bismark

Hunting the Bismarck was Forester's last non-Hornblower book. In fact, it did not begin as an historical study, but rather as the commissioned screenplay for the motion picture *Sink the Bismarck!* (words spoken, perhaps unnecessarily, by Winston Churchill in the book). Forester turned the screenplay into a serial for the *Saturday Evening Post* and then into a book. The marks of an adapted screenplay are quite apparent in the scenelike, episodal structure; the quick cutting back and forth among the various scenes of action such as the British Admiralty War Room, the bridges of various combatant vessels, a radio announcer's studio in New York City, and other places; the omission of chapter divisions; and the "recreated" dialogue. For, as Forester states in a two-sentence introduction, "this is as it may have happened. The speeches are composed by the writer, who has no knowledge that those words were used; but the writer has no doubt that similar speeches were made."[17]

Furthermore, the tone of the book is sensational; it is primed with heavy charges of melodrama and sentimentality. Reviewers correctly did not treat the new work as serious history. Forester's research was limited and cursory. Although he did interview British participants in the sinking of the *Bismarck*, he did not communicate with any of the approximately 100 German survivors. As a result, the German actions are more vague and speculative than are those of the British, and there are actually historical errors. Although the time is mid-May of 1941, Forester has the German Captain Lindemann receive the award of the "Knights Cross with Swords and Diamonds," whereas the award was not created by Hitler until 1943. Young officers cheer the stirring words of a "political officer," but political officers were not assigned to German ships until after the Bomb Plot against Hitler in 1944.[18]

However, it was high drama that Forester was after and not primary history, and in that aim he succeeded. The book is entirely cleared for action, with little emphasis on the naval details which Forester relished in all of his previous nautical writings. Thus *Hunting the Bismarck* is only 138 pages long; the writing is journalistically lean; it is rather like a long story without a single structural division such as a chapter. *Hunting the Bismarck* sweeps forward, like the dreadnought it memorializes, from the first to the last word of the book.

Hunting the Bismarck deals with the nine days in May 1941 in which the *Bismarck* left her home port in Gdynia in order to destroy the British convoy system and effect an end to the war by the disruption of British supplies. As the world's largest and fastest battleship, the *Bismarck*, theoretically, could effect such a strategic decision, if she could avoid meeting concentrations of the British battleship fleet.

At first the *Bismarck* is amazingly fortunate and successful. The weather closes in and British air reconnaissance is unable to find the enemy dreadnought, while the *Bismarck* with her fine radar is able to move at will. Then the *Bismarck* encounters the old battle-cruiser *Hood* and the brand-new but untested battleship *Prince of Wales* in the Denmark Strait. The *Bismarck* blows up the *Hood* with almost her first volley. She then severely damages the *Prince of Wales,* who breaks off contact and flees for life.

The *Bismarck* has been slightly damaged; her fuel capacity and thus her range have been impaired. Admiral Lutjens, whom Forester portrays as a stereotypical, fanatical Nazi leader, decides to take the ship to the French port of Brest for minor repairs before continuing the cruise. Almost the entire British North Sea, Atlantic, and Mediterranean fleets converge on the *Bismarck* in order to prevent her reaching German air cover from France. All convoys are stripped of large escorts. Churchill orders that the Bismarck must be sunk, but her escape seems unavoidable until the British, whose luck has been appalling, see destiny seeming to reverse itself and the wheel of chance make a favorable turn. A British Swordfish torpedo bomber from the carrier *Ark Royal* scores a lucky hit on the rudder of the *Bismarck* and the behemoth looses steering control and much of her speed. The British battleships reach her just before she can come under Luftwaffe cover and they pound the German ship to pieces. Finally, destroyers send her, the admiral, her captain, and almost her entire crew to the bottom with *coup de grace* torpedoes. Several thousand British and German sailors died, but the British avoided a major strategic defeat and won permanent control of the surface of the Atlantic Ocean and the North Sea.

From the beginning, Forester sets a tone of high seriousness in language that borders on the melodramatic:

This is a story of the most desperate chances, of the loftiest patriotism and of the highest professional skills, of a gamble for the dominion of the world in which human lives were the stakes on the green gaming table of the ocean. There was a pursuit without precedent in the history of navies; there were battles fought in which the defeated gained as much glory as the victors, and in which the most unpredictable bad luck was counterbalanced by miraculous good fortune. For six days that pursuit lasted, days of un-relenting storm, of tossing gray seas and lowering clouds, without a single gleam of sunshine to lighten the setting of the background of tragedy. Those actors in the tragedy who played their parts at sea did so to the unceasing accompaniment of shrieking wind, leaping waves, flying spray, and bitter cold.

And all this took place against a background of events of vital importance in the history of the world, when England stood alone, almost ringed-in by enemies of unbelievable power and malignity. She was friendless and yet unafraid, guarded and vigilant. . . .[19]

As in *The Ship* and *The Good Shepherd*, Forester is masterful in his accurate and detailed description of modern naval war in the North Atlantic. His account of the death of H.M.S. *Hood* is unmatched in his historical prose as he weaves personal observation by participants with the facts:

First there was the silhouette of the ship, sharp and clear now that she had emerged entirely from the mist. Then from somewhere just forward of the funnel came a jet of thick gray smoke. But before this had finished its course, before it had begun to mushroom out, a dozen other jets of smoke, each larger than the first, burst from the ship, expanding so that close above the ship they united, still soaring upwards and still expanding to form a dense cloud hanging over the ship from a great height, attached to it by a vague and slender stalk. It was in that moment that Lindemann, through his excellent binoculars, believed he could see great fragments of the ship soaring upwards to the cloud, outstripped by the jets at first but reaching the smoke now that it was nearly stationary. And he was nearly sure that he saw bow and stern of the ship rise up out of the water and the waist sink, as though a wonton child had seized a bathtub toy and snapped it across the middle.

It was only for that moment that Lindemann saw this. The broken-backed toy was instantly engulfed in further smoke, pouring from every aperture in the ship, lying low on the surface so that there was nothing to be seen except the few brief splashes as the high-tossed fragments of masts and decks and armor plate came arrowing back into the sea. And when this lower pall of smoke lifted and thinned there was nothing to be seen. Nothing.

And of Nobby and his friends in the turret there was nothing. One moment they had been hard at work, bending and heaving in the hard harsh light of the electric lamps; they were boxed up in their little room, separated from the world around them and above them by armor plate of steel a foot thick; below them the deep sea—below them the magazine and shellroom and three hundred tons of high explosive. For one moment it had been thus; the next, and the shell which *Bismarck* had sent hurtling towards them had crashed its way, as though endowed with a malignant intelligence, through half a dozen decks, half a dozen bulkheads, through the chink in Hood's armour, along the narrow unguarded route to the magazine below the turret, there to burst among those three hundred tons of high explosive. In that second, Nobby and his friends passed, without a chance of knowing it, from existence to annihilation.[20]

The damage to the *Prince of Wales* is described in vivid cinematic images:

The whole bridge was a mass of flaming wreckage and heaped corpses. In the chartroom below, the navigating officer saw something drip out of the voice-pipe onto the chart before him.
"What on earth?" He put his hand out and touched it. "My God, it's blood!" It went on dropping thickly down upon the chart.
Upon the bridge a tattered, smoke-blackened figure crawled to the voice-pipe and pulled aside the corpse which lay across the mouth.
"Hard a-port. Steer one-five-o. Hard a-port."
"Hard a-port," repeated the navigating officer in the chartroom. The ship heeled violently as the helm went over, so that the navigating officer had to hold on to save himself.
Far in the depths of the turret down in the traverse space the heel was felt and the men had to hold on. There was a clatter and crash and the ring slipped from its rollers and crashed over lopsided. A shell slid off and trapped the civilian worker there by the leg with its three-quarters-of-a-ton weight. He cried out with pain. As the shell crew turned to help him he forced himself to speak normally.
"All right, chums. Tell 'em up above the ring's jammed. Y turret won't fire until you've cleared it," The shell moved a little on his leg.
"A-ah," he said in agony, and fainted.[12]

Forester fans were not disappointed with *Hunting the Bismarck*, even if the critics were. The author managed to pack into a short book a full measure of suspense; a terrible fear of the power of evil even if the reader is quite aware from the beginning that the evil is doomed; a large dose of British patriotism; even a little American pride due to the brief appearance of a United States Navy lieutenant on the battleship H.M.S. *Rodney*; and a sense of satisfaction with the plans and machinations of human destiny. Forester's last historical and last non-Hornblower book left his popular audience with the belief that his creative powers were undiminished.

The three non-Hornblower books of Forester's last period of work proved, if ever there was a doubt, that the author was a master wordsmith who was equally at home in World War II naval history or fiction, as well as in fictional and nonfictional subjects relating to naval matters in the Napoleonic period and the early nineteenth century in general. One can only speculate that better health and thus longer life would have found C. S. Forester concentrating more on works that further implied the significance of sea power on the history of the West in the hope of seeing the NATO Navy remain the master of the world's sea lanes. He was an initial consultant on the "Victory at Sea" TV series. Further World War II naval novels as well as film and TV scripts might have made it politically possible, through increased popular support, for the United States to have a far larger navy in the last quarter of the twentieth century.

CHAPTER 8

Achievement and Summation

C. S. Forester was and is one of the most popular novelists of the twentieth century. Over 8 million copies of his books have been sold to date. Serialized during three decades, his fiction reached millions through the *Saturday Evening Post* and other general periodicals. Six of his books, *Brown on Resolution* (film title: *Born for Glory*), *The African Queen*, *The Gun* (film title: *The Pride and the Passion*), *Payment Deferred*, *Hunting the Bismarck* (film title: *Sink the Bismarck*), and *Beat to Quarters* (film title: *Captain Horatio Hornblower*), were made into motion pictures, with the award-winning *African Queen* apparently destined for film immortality. All the Hornblower books remain in paperback print at this writing and they appear to garner new enthusiasts with succeeding generations.

The critical reader cannot compare Forester's limited intentions with those of the great early-twentieth-century English novelists in their most significant works, nearly contemporary with Forester's initial efforts as a novelist: E. M. Forster's *A Passage to India* (1924), James Joyce's *A Portrait of the Artist as a Young Man* (1916) and *Ulysses* (1922), and Virginia Woolf's *To the Lighthouse* (1927). These worthier but more esoteric novels appealed to a highly critical, better educated, more serious, but less numerous audience. Forester was never in their league, nor even in that of Evelyn Waugh, Aldous Huxley, or George Orwell, nor did he seem to wish to be.

C. S. Forester was, first of all, a storyteller. He provided, during pre-television and even early television days, a "jolly good read." His carefully researched, finely plotted, highly melodramatic novels provided and still provide a great amount of pleasure to readers desiring to escape for a while from their humdrum lives into a romanticized past. Britons, seeing the decline of their once omnipotent empire as well as the wartime decimation of their young manhood, took solace in the exploits of Horatio Hornblower as he

159

tweaked the nose of the tyrant Bonaparte during the high glory of the English nation and the Royal Navy. Their American cousins somewhat more vicariously enjoyed the fun and nostalgia, too. On a more serious note, and not to be overlooked, is the fact that the Hornblower Saga turned out to be a piece of much-needed "propaganda" for the British and perhaps for the Allies in general during the dark hours just before and at the beginning of the Second World War. Afterwards, during continued rationing and readjustments, Hornblower, happily, was there, too. At the time of great military and even greater political defeats (and some victories, too) for Britain, one fictional Englishman, a man of intelligence, courage, compassion, integrity, and great resourcefulness, rose to do battle, successfully, with a seemingly multi-headed monster, and all English-speaking people took heart. If Hornblower and the wooden ships of the Royal Navy (echoes of Nelson) could thwart the ambitions of Napoleon, could not contemporary Britons and Americans destroy Hitler and the Nazi tyranny? Could they not also face and defeat the enemies in the Cold War? Horatio Hornblower was a kind of "real" war hero after all.

I   *Growth and Development*

In the Platonic literary world created by hermeneutics, there is little room for C. S. Forester. His early work, divided between hack biographies which he despised, and weakly contrived, caricature-ridden novels, showed little promise and seemed to indicate a writer who was oblivious to all that was happening about him in his own time, whether in the realm of art or in the social and historical milieu. He never joined a "school" of literature or a salon and never made a close friend of any other young English novelist. There was much for Forester to overcome. He had to grow and mature into the outstanding historical novelist he would become. As a young man he seemed as much interested in living the Bohemian life of a writer as he was in seriously pursuing his craft. Not that he did not work hard. His early output was staggering, but as he did not come from a literary background and had had no training at writing, he very much needed to study his craft more than he did. Furthermore, his inclinations were toward becoming a historian. He loved a certain kind of history, the high drama of war and great political events. War itself, the experience he had both luckily and unluckily missed, fascinated him, so that all of his best writing would relate to the experience of men and women either in combat or under the stress and compulsion of war.

Essentially a political conservative, Forester grew to hate totalitarianism, perhaps as a result of his observation of the Spanish Civil War. His early admiration for Napoleon turned to dislike as he transferred his growing antagonism for Mussolini, as evidenced in *The Ship*, and for Hitler, as indicated in *The Ship* and *The Good Shepherd*, as well as many of the stories in *The Nightmare* and *The Man in the Yellow Raft*, to Napoleon in the Hornblower Saga. A major theme in Forester's work developed as he began to leave behind the psychological novels and the biographies. The Man Alone theme permitted Forester to examine human nature in a manner similar to the way Ernest Hemingway often viewed it. The latter's admiration for "grace under pressure" was not dissimilar to Forester's contention that unrelieved pressure in a situation where the leader, unaided, made life-and-death decisions brought out the best in a human being and could even make an ordinary person rise to deeds of great heroism and self-sacrifice regardless of the nature of the cause he was serving. Its fictional beginnings are to be found in *Brown on Resolution*, and both the Hornblower Saga and *The Good Shepherd* represent the ultimate exploration of this theme by Forester.

II *Achievement*

As a propagandist, perhaps an unconscious one, C. S. Forester contributed significantly to the Anglo-American alliance from 1939 to the present day. His fiction and his historical studies convinced millions of readers of the importance of maintaining sea power supremacy. If the British could no longer afford it, then it was up to the Americans to keep the sea lanes open for the Free World.

Forester contributed to a growing British nostalgia for past glories and the days of the Empire. A contributing factor to Hornblower's great popularity is the fact that he is a figure of the pre–industrial revolution and the pre-Victorian past, a product of an earlier, seemingly simpler time. Unlike a more contemporary fantasy hero, James Bond, Hornblower is less dependent upon machines. His engines are muscle-powered and wind-moved. Hornblower does not act alone. He leads men. He brings them to battery. He causes them to see and do their duty. It is no accident that Ian Fleming's hero, James Bond, succeeded Hornblower as the prototype British hero.

Hornblower, a product of World War II, is a hero to lead masses. Bond, a product of the Cold War and a more narcissistic, more individualistic period, works alone, is cynical, and is far more interested in his personal pleasure than is the self-sacrificing and duty-seeking Hornblower. Perhaps because they were so much attuned to the consciousness of their times, Hornblower and Bond have developed "historical existences" and have become part of the language and the collective "experience" of the contemporary Western world.

C. S. Forester wrote three superb novels outside of the Hornblower Saga: *The General, The African Queen,* and *The Good Shepherd.* Their excellence and their popularity are due to the fineness of Forester's characterization, the superbly controlled plotting, the painstaking attention to detail, the clarity of style, and the holistic concept of the novel form that reduced each book to a state of muscular leanness. Forester's best work, like the author himself, was always in fighting trim.

Furthermore, these three novels each focus on either one or two principals and make no pretense of further extended characterizations. Each protagonist is presented with a choice, not a moral choice between right and wrong, but one between duty and self. In the struggles of the protagonists to choose while never fully comprehending that they have a choice and must make it, lies much of the fascination of these novels. Of course the protagonists of *The African Queen* and *The Good Shepherd* choose duty and are rewarded with survival, self-satisfaction, and expanded souls. General Curzon, however, a basically stupid man, chooses self as he deludes himself into believing that he is choosing duty. His end is therefore tragic and the results and consequences of his actions are catastrophic for the British people.

III *Influence*

Forester brought the romantic historical novel to a near pinnacle in the twentieth century. Only Margaret Mitchell's *Gone With the Wind* (1936) appealed to the Anglo-American collective consciousness as did the Hornblower Saga, and much of Mitchell's impact came through the enormous popularity of the film version. His ultimate achievement for the general readership may be that, like Mitchell, he brilliantly recreated a past time and place and gave birth to a protagonist worthy of such a background.

Naturally the success of the Hornblower Saga spawned imitators. None could approach the originality, force, and verisimilitude of the model. Even Forester's American imitation of Hornblower, perhaps intended to create a nostalgic nineteenth-century American prototypical hero, Captain Peabody in *Captain from Connecticut*, did not succeed, partly because, unlike the declining Great Britain, the United States was not ready for that kind of emotional indulgence, but mainly because the original was too strong, too pervasive, too skillful to permit successful imitation.

Other successful historical novelists, working concurrently with Forester or following him on the literary scene, such as Howard Fast, James Michener, and especially John Jakes with his Kent Family Chronicles in *The Americans* series, may sell more books and earn more money than did Forester, but none seems to have created a cult readership partially based on admiration for a recurring protagonist.

In all probability, even C. S. Forester's stronger non-Hornblower novels, *The General*, *The African Queen*, and *The Good Shepherd*, will continue to be read as fallout from the Hornblower Saga by readers introduced to the author with the Saga and desiring to read additional pleasurable work by the same writer. They will not be disappointed. In the specific case of *The African Queen*, the continued popularity of the Humphrey Bogart–Katharine Hepburn film will assure a readership for many future years. Many of these future readers will be pleasantly surprised by both the content and the depth of these novels. They will find in *The General* a disturbing but eminently valuable dissection of the military mind. In *The African Queen* they will admire the resources available in seemingly the most ordinary of human beings. In *The Good Shepherd* they will learn that courage, self-sacrifice, and devotion to duty above self-interest remain desirable human qualities. If C. S. Forester broke no new ground in these works, he at least reaffirmed insights and values of use to men and women of the last decades of this century and the beginning of the next.

However, it is as a purveyor of popular literature that C. S. Forester will be remembered most frequently, just as Robert Frost is largely remembered for a few moving poems and John Masefield for *Salt-Water Ballads*. These twentieth-century writers, like Forester, will be superficially read and enjoyed by the mass audience, while their more profound work will appeal to a more limited and more erudite audience, but that other work is always there for those who wish to delve more deeply and read the artists' philosophical and intellectual premises, and even, perhaps, their souls.

Hornblower sails on.

Notes and References

Chapter One

1. *New York Times*, April 3, 1966, p. 84.
2. "Hornblower and I," *Saturday Evening Post*, May 11, 1957, p. 141.
3. Ibid.
4. *Long Before Forty* (Boston: Little, Brown, 1967), p. 7.
5. Ibid., p. 8.
6. Ibid.
7. Ibid., p. 13.
8. Ibid., p. 14.
9. Ibid., p. 15.
10. Ibid.
11. Ibid., p. 16.
12. Ibid., pp. 16–17.
13. "Hornblower's Creator—An Englishman in California," *Newsweek*, July 9, 1956, p. 104.
14. *Long Before Forty*, pp. 22–23.
15. Ibid., pp. 24–28.
16. Ibid., pp. 30–31.
17. Ibid., p. 32.
18. Ibid., p. 49.
19. Ibid., p. 71.
20. Ibid., p. 75.
21. Ibid., pp. 78–79.
22. Ibid., p. 79.
23. Ibid.
24. Ibid., p. 80.
25. Ibid., p. 82.
26. Ibid.
27. Ibid., p. 83.
28. Ibid., p. 84.
29. Ibid., p. 94.
30. Ibid., p. 95.
31. Ibid., p. 100.
32. Ibid., p. 117.
33. Ibid., p. 118.
34. Ibid., p. 119.
35. "Talk with the Author," *Newsweek*, September 1, 1958, p. 58.
36. *Long Before Forty*, p. 120.
37. Ibid., p. 125.

38. Ibid., p. 126.
39. Ibid., p. 123.
40. Ibid., pp. 137–40.
41. Ibid., p. 159.
42. Ibid., p. 166.
43. Ibid., p. 167.
44. Ibid., p. 171.
45. Ibid., p. 167.
46. *The General* (Boston: Little, Brown, 1947), preface.
47. Ibid.
48. Ibid.
49. *The Hornblower Companion* (Boston: Little, Brown, 1964), p. 109.
50. Ibid., p. 107.
51. Ibid.
52. Ibid., p. 109.
53. Ibid., p. 111.
54. Ibid., p. 113.
55. Ibid., p. 114.
56. Ibid., p. 117.
57. Ibid., p. 120.
58. "I Can't Walk," *Saturday Evening Post*, April 21, 1946, p. 19.
59. Ibid., p. 99.
60. Ibid.
61. "Last of Hornblower," *Saturday Evening Post*, July 6, 1946, p. 4.
62 "Talk with the Author," *Newsweek*, September 1, 1958, p. 57.
63 "The Trouble with Travel," *Saturday Evening Post*, November 28, 1959, pp. 42, 65–67.
64 "Talk with the Author," *Newsweek*, September 1, 1958, p. 57.
65. *The Hornblower Companion*, p. 99.
66. Ibid., p. 103.
67. Ibid., p. 104.
68. Ibid., p. 170.
69. Ibid., p. 74.
70. *Long Before Forty*, p. 172.

Chapter Two

1. *Long Before Forty*, pp. 119–20.
2. Ibid., pp. 122–23.
3. *The Paid Piper* (London: Methuen, 1924), p. 12.
4. Ibid., p. 50.
5. Ibid., p. 47.
6. Ibid., p. 38.
7. Ibid., pp. 149–50.

8. Ibid., pp. 174–75.
9. Ibid., pp. 173–74.
10. Ibid., p. 41.
11. *Long Before Forty*, p. 129.
12. *A Pawn among Kings* (London: Methuen, 1924), p. 116.
13. Ibid., p. 191.
14. Ibid., p. 99.
15. *Payment Deferred* (Boston: Little, Brown, 1942), p. 97.
16. *The Wonderful Week* (London: John Lane The Bodley Head, 1927), p. 2.
17. Ibid., p. 180.
18. Ibid., p. 11.
19. Ibid., p. 312.
20. Ibid., p. 161.
21. *Plain Murder* (London: The Bodley Head, 1967), p. 10.
22. Ibid., p. 142.
23. *Love Lies Dreaming* (Indianapolis: Bobbs-Merrill, 1927), p. 72.
24. Ibid., p. 26.
25. Ibid., p. 32.
26. *The Daughter of the Hawk* (Indianapolis: Bobbs-Merrill, 1928), pp. 48–49.
27. *Long Before Forty*, p. 149.
28. *The Daughter of the Hawk*, p. 210.
29. Ibid., p. 273.
30. *Brown on Resolution* (London: John Lane The Bodley Head, 1929), p. 5.
31. Fred T. Jane, *Jane's Fighting Ships 1914* (London: S. Low, Marston, 1914), p. 75.
32. *Brown on Resolution*, p. 92.
33. Ibid., p. 12.
34. Ibid., p. 175.
35. *Two and Twenty* (London: John Lane The Bodley Head, 1931), p. 22.
36. Ibid., pp. 76–78.
37. *Long Before Forty*, p. 147.
38. Ibid.
39. *Napoleon and His Court* (New York: Dodd, Mead, 1924), p. 10.
40. *Long Before Forty*, p. 152.
41. *Josephine: Napoleon's Empress* (New York: Dodd, Mead, 1925), p. 1.
42. Ibid., pp. 121–22.
43. Ibid., pp. 193–94.
44. *Victor Emmanuel II and the Union of Italy* (New York: Dodd, Mead, 1927), pp. 3–4.
45. Ibid., p. 8.

46. Ibid., p. 222.
47. *Louis XIV: King of France and Navarre* (New York: Dodd, Mead, 1928), p. 192.
48. Ibid., pp. 152, 159–60, 163–64, 168.
49. Ibid., p. 163.
50. Ibid., p. 172.
51. Ibid., p. 171.
52. *Lord Nelson* (Indianapolis: Bobbs-Merrill, 1929), pp. 11–12, 21.
53. Ibid., p. 272.
54. *The Voyage of the "Annie Marble"* (London: John Lane The Bodley Head, 1929), p. 22.
55. Ibid., pp. 19–20.
56. Ibid., p. 40.
57. Ibid., p. 7.
58. Ibid., pp. 206–208.
59. *The "Annie Marble" in Germany* (London: John Lane The Bodley Head, 1930), p. 75.
60. Ibid., p. 87.

Chapter Three

1. *Rifleman Dodd and the Gun* (New York: The Readers Club, 1942), p. 181.
2. Ibid., p. viii.
3. *New York Times Book Review*, August 27, 1933, p. 13.
4. *Rifleman Dodd and the Gun*, pp. 28–29.
5. *The Peacemaker* (London: Heinemann, 1934), p. 42.
6. Ibid., p. 36.
7. Harvey Breit, "Talk with C. S. Forester," *New York Times Book Review*, April 6, 1952, p. 16.
8. Ibid.
9. Percy Hutchinson, "A Strange Wartime Adventure in German East Africa," *New York Times Book Review*, February 10, 1935, p. 5.
10. See J. R. Sibley, *Tanganyikan Guerrilla: East African Campaigns 1914–1918* (New York: Ballantine, 1971).
11. *The African Queen* (London: Heinemann, 1935), pp. 163–64.
12. Sibley, pp. 77–81.
13. Arthur Loveman, "Mad Adventure," *Saturday Review of Literature*, February 9, 1935, p. 473.
14. *The African Queen*, p. 183.
15. Ibid., p. 184.
16. Ibid., p. 85.
17. Ibid., p. 21.
18. Ibid., pp. 13–14.

19. Ibid., p. 14.
20. Ibid., p. 15.
21. John Ellis, *The Social History of the Machine Gun* (New York: Pantheon, 1975), p. 62.
22. B. H. Liddell-Hart, *The Tanks* (London: Cassell, 1959), I, 234.
23. Louis Kronenberger, "A Modern Major General," *Nation*, April 1, 1936, p. 421.
24. *The General*, pp. 53–54.
25. *Nation*, April 1, 1936, p. 421.
26. Robert van Gelder, "Author of 'Captain Horatio Hornblower,'" *New York Times Book Review*, February 23, 1941, p. 2.

Chapter Four

1. *The Hornblower Companion*, p. 107.
2. John K. Hutchens, "On an Author," *New York Herald Tribune*, March 30, 1952, p. 2.
3. *Hornblower and the Atropos*, in *The Young Hornblower* (London: Michael Joseph, 1964), p. 428.
4. *The Hornblower Companion*, pp. 171–72.
5. The naval historian C. Northcote Parkinson, using the events of Forester's Hornblower Saga as a basis, wrote a "documented biography" of *The Life and Times of Horatio Hornblower* (1970). Parkinson has Hornblower die in 1857 and Lady Barbara die in 1861.
6. *The Autobiography of a Seaman*, Two Volumes (London: R. Bentley, 1860).
7. *Thomas, Lord Cochrane*, Two Volumes (London: R. Bentley, 1869).
8. For a new biography of Cochrane, see Donald Thomas, *Cochrane: Britannia's Last Sea-King* (New York: Viking, 1979).
9. *The Hornblower Companion*, p. 111.
10. Ibid., p. 114.
11. Ibid., p. 124.

Chapter Five

1. *To the Indies* (Boston: Little, Brown, 1940), pp. 197–98.
2. Ibid., p. 212.
3. *Saturday Review*, July 27, 1940, p. 5.
4. Drake DeKay, *New York Times Book Review*, June 15, 1941, p. 7.
5. *The Captain from Connecticut*, (Boston: Little, Brown, 1941), p. 344.
6. *Christian Science Monitor*, June 17, 1941, p. 20.
7. *The Captain from Connecticut*, pp. 289–90.

8. Howard Mumford Jones, *Saturday Review*, June 14, 1941.
9. *Nation*, June 5, 1943, p. 316.
10. *The Ship* (Boston: Little, Brown, 1943), pp. 21–22.
11. Ibid., pp. 140–42.

Chapter Six

1. *The Sky and the Forest* (Boston: Little, Brown, 1948), p. 313.
2. Ibid., pp. 265–67.
3. Ibid., pp. 15–16.
4. Miles Edwin Greene, "A Tale of Imperialism in the Congo," *New York Times Book Review*, August 15, 1948, p. 5.
5. See Hollis Alpert, "Chief of the Congo," *Saturday Review*, August 14, 1948, pp. 19–20.
6. *Randall and the River of Time* (Boston: Little, Brown, 1950), pp. 24–25.
7. Walter Havighurst, "Young Man without Water Wings," *Saturday Review*, December 16, 1950, p. 12.
8. *Times Literary Supplement*, January 19, 1951, p. 33.
9. *Randall and the River of Time*, pp. 6–7.
10. Ibid., pp. 170–71.
11. Ibid., pp. 92–93.
12. Ibid., p. 341.
13. *Times Literary Supplement*, January 19, 1951, p. 33.

Chapter Seven

1. *The Good Shepherd* (Boston: Little, Brown, 1955), p. 32.
2. Ibid., p. 33.
3. Ibid., p. 34.
4. Ibid., p. 83.
5. Ibid., pp. 123–24.
6. Ibid., p. 210.
7. Ibid., p. 216.
8. Ibid., p. 310.
9. Burke Wilkinson, "With the Wolf Pack Dead Ahead," *New York Times Book Review*, March 27, 1955, p. 1.
10. Roland Sawyer, *Christian Science Monitor*, July 5, 1956, p. 7.
11. *The Age of Fighting Sail* (New York: Doubleday, 1956), p. 22.
12. Henry F. Groff, "Brave Ships, Iron Men," *New York Times Book Review*, July 8, 1956, p. 7.
13. *The Age of Fighting Sail*, p. 125.
14. Ibid., p. 61.

15. Ibid., p. 246.
16. Groff, "Brave Ships," p. 70.
17. *The Last Nine Days of the Bismarck* (Boston: Little, Brown, 1959), p. 2.
18. "Voyage to Destruction," *New York Times Book Review*, April 5, 1959, p. 14.
19. *The Last Nine Days of the Bismarck*, pp. 3–4.
20. Ibid., pp. 51–53.
21. Ibid., pp. 58–59.

Selected Bibliography

PRIMARY SOURCES

A Pawn among Kings. London: Methuen, 1924.

Napoleon and His Court. London: Methuen, 1924.

The Paid Piper. London: Methuen, 1924.

Josephine, Napoleon's Empress. London: Methuen, 1925; New York: Dodd, Mead, 1925.

Payment Deferred. London: John Lane The Bodley Head, 1926; Boston: Little, Brown, 1942.

Love Lies Dreaming. London: John Lane The Bodley Head, 1927; Indianapolis: Bobbs-Merrill, 1927.

Victor Emmanuel II and the Union of Italy. London: Methuen, 1927; New York: Dodd, Mead, 1927.

The Wonderful Week. London: John Lane The Bodley Head, 1927; Indianapolis: Bobbs-Merrill, 1927 (as *One Wonderful Week*).

Louis XIV, King of France and Navarre. London: Methuen, 1928; New York: Dodd, Mead, 1928.

The Shadow of the Hawk. London: John Lane the Bodley Head, 1928; Indianapolis: Bobbs-Merrill, 1928 (as *The Daughter of the Hawk*).

Brown on Resolution. London: John Lane the Bodley Head, 1929; New York: Putnam, 1929 (as *Singlehanded*).

The Voyage of the "Annie Marble." London: John Lane The Bodley Head, 1929.

Nelson. London: John Lane The Bodley Head, 1929; Indianapolis: Bobbs-Merrill, 1929 (as *Lord Nelson*).

The "Annie Marble" in Germany. London: John Lane The Bodley Head, 1930.

Plain Murder. London: John Lane The Bodley Head, 1930; New York: Dell Publishing, 1954.

U-97: A Play in Three Acts. London: John Lane The Bodley Head, 1931.

Two and Twenty. London: John Lane The Bodley Head, 1931; New York: Appleton, 1931.

Death to the French. London: John Lane The Bodley Head, 1932; New York: The Readers Club, 1942 (as *Rifleman Dodd in Rifleman Dodd and the Gun: Two Novels of the Peninsular Wars*).

The Gun. London: John Lane The Bodley Head, 1933; Boston: Little, Brown, 1933.

Nurse Cavell: A Play in Three Acts. London: John Lane The Bodley Head, 1933. With C. E. Bechofer Roberts.

The Peacemaker. London: Heinemann, 1934; Boston: Little, Brown, 1934.

The African Queen. London: Heinemann, 1935; Boston: Little, Brown, 1935.

Marionettes at Home. London: Michael Joseph, 1936.

The General. London: Michael Joseph, 1936; Boston: Little, Brown, 1936.

The Happy Return. London: Michael Joseph, 1937; Boston: Little, Brown, 1937 (as *Beat to Quarters*).

A Ship of the Line. London: Michael Joseph, 1938; Boston: Little, Brown, 1938 (as *Ship of the Line*).

Flying Colours. London: Michael Joseph, 1938; Boston: Little, Brown, 1938.

The Earthly Paradise. London: Michael Joseph, 1940; Boston: Little, Brown, 1940 (as *To the Indies*).

The Captain from Connecticut. London: Michael Joseph, 1941; Boston: Little, Brown, 1941.

Poo-Poo and the Dragons. London: Michael Joseph, 1942; Boston: Little, Brown, 1942.

The Ship. London: Michael Joseph, 1943; Boston: Little, Brown, 1943.

The Bedchamber Mystery. Toronto: S. J. Reginald Saunders, 1944.

The Commodore. London; Michael Joseph, 1945; Boston: Little, Brown, 1945 (as *Commodore Hornblower*).

Lord Hornblower. London: Michael Joseph, 1946; Boston: Little, Brown, 1946.

The Sky and the Forest. London: Michael Joseph, 1948; Boston: Little, Brown, 1948.

Mr. Midshipman Hornblower. London: Michael Joseph, 1950; Boston: Little, Brown, 1950.

Randall and the River of Time. Boston: Little, Brown, 1950; London: Michael Joseph, 1951.

Lieutenant Hornblower. London: Michael Joseph, 1952; Boston: Little, Brown, 1952.

The Barbary Pirates. New York: Random House, 1953; London: Macdonald, 1956.

Hornblower and the Atropos. London: Michael Joseph, 1953; Boston: Little, Brown, 1953.

The Nightmare. London: Michael Joseph, 1954; Boston: Little, Brown, 1954.

The Good Shepherd. London: Michael Joseph, 1955; Boston: Little, Brown, 1955.

The Age of Fighting Sail. Garden City, N.Y.: Doubleday, 1956; London: Michael Joseph, 1957 (as *The Naval War of 1812*).

Hornblower in the West Indies. London: Michael Joseph,1958; Boston: Little, Brown, 1958 (as *Admiral Hornblower in the West Indies*).

Hunting the Bismarck. London: Michael Joseph, 1959; Boston: Little Brown, 1959 (as *The Last Nine Days of the Bismarck*).

Hornblower and the Hotspur. London: Michael Joseph, 1962; Boston: Little, Brown, 1962.
The Hornblower Companion. London: Michael Joseph, 1964; Boston: Little, Brown, 1964.
Hornblower and the Crisis. London: Michael Joseph, 1967; Boston: Little, Brown, 1967 (as *Hornblower during the Crisis*).
Long Before Forty. London: Michael Joseph, 1967; Boston: Little, Brown, 1968.
The Man in the Yellow Raft. London: Michael Joseph, 1969; Boston: Little, Brown, 1969.
Gold from Crete. Boston: Little, Brown, 1970; London: Michael Joseph, 1971.

SECONDARY SOURCES

Forester, John, "Father's Tales." *American Scholar,* vol. 66 (Fall 1997), 533–545. A memoir of a difficult relationship.
Fultz, James R. "A Classic Case of Collaboration: The African Queen." *Film-Literature-Quarterly* 1982, 10:1, 13–24. Film's success due in large part to collaboration between author, director, and screen writer.
Hornblower—One More Time. Tacoma, Washington: The Richard Bolitho Association, 1976. Contains three Hornblower stories previously published only in magazines, a Hornblower chronology, and a Forester bibliography by William Orobko. A useful book, but unfortunately only 350 copies were published.
"The Great Man." Unpublished biography of C. S. Forester by his son, John Forester.
Perrett, Bryan. *The Real Hornblower: The Life of Admiral of the Fleet Sir James Alexander Gordon, GCB.* Annapolis, Md.: Naval Institute Press, 1997.

Index